SMART COOKIES

80 Recipes for Heavenly, Healthful Snacking

JANE KINDERLEHRER

Illustrations by Claude Martinot

NEWMARKET PRESS

New York

The Newmarket Jane Kinderlehrer Smart Food Series

To the very special Smart Cookies
who raid my cookie jar—
Jodi, Becca, Lisa, Hannah, Aaron, Eliana,
Sammie, Tova, Janie, and Noah.

Copyright © 1985 Jane Kinderlehrer

This book published simultaneously
in the United States of America and in Canada.

First Edition
4 5 6 7 8 9 0

Library of Congress Cataloging in Publication Data

Kinderlehrer, Jane.
  Smart cookies.

  Includes index.
  1. Cookies.   2. Cookery (Natural foods)   I. Title.
  TX772.K56   1985   641.8′654   85-13913
  ISBN 0-937858-62-5 (pbk.)

Quantity Purchases
Companies, professional groups, clubs and other organizations may qualify for
special terms when ordering quantities of this title. For information contact: Special
Sales Dept., Newmarket Press, 18 East 48th Street, New York, New York 10017,
or call (212) 832-3575.

Designed by Ruth Kolbert
Manufactured in the United States of America

Contents

METRIC CONVERSION CHART

1 teaspoon = 5 ml.   1 tablespoon = 15 ml.
1 ounce = 30 ml.   1 cup = 240 ml./.24 l.
1 quart = 950 ml./.95 l.   1 gallon = 3.80 l.

1 ounce = 28 gr.   1 pound = 454 gr./.454 kg.

F.°	200	225	250	275	300	325	350	375	400	425	450
C.°	93	107	121	135	149	163	177	191	204	218	232

INTRODUCTION

There's nothing like a cookie. A cookie cheers you when you're blue, keeps you company when you're lonely, keeps you from smoking. They're not very strong, but they can break the ice at a party. They go well with milk, tea, coffee, or lemonade, and they're nice to share with family, friends, and Fido.

There are times when we don't feel like eating a regular meal, or don't have the time to eat, or don't know what to eat. But who can refuse a cookie? Even a high-chair thumper who won't eat her Pablum will eat a cookie.

The problem with most cookies, though, is that they can make you fat, decay your teeth, give you a bellyache, and send you on a guilt trip. Smart Cookies are different—oh, so deliciously different. They're absolutely great for squelching the "I wants" and the "Gimmes," and marvelous for breaking the junk food habit because they have *no* empty calories.

Empty calories, such as those you get from refined sugar and bleached white flour, contain no body-nurturing nutrients—only fat-producing calories. Empty calories need vitamin B (especially B1, or thiamine) to be metabolized in your body. If you consume much sugar, and most of us do since it's hidden in so many of the commercial foods we buy, you're likely to suffer a deficiency in B1, which leads to fatigue, depression, and neuritis (pains in the joints).

Smart Cookies are dense in nutrients, each programmed to do a special job, without the abundance of fat and refined sweeteners found in ordinary cookies. They're rich in the vitamin B group to nourish your nerves and put a sparkle in your eyes; rich in calcium to strengthen your bones; rich in iron for your blood; rich in fiber to keep your colon healthy; rich in potassium for your heart; and chock-full of many other nutrients which I will tell you about with each recipe.

In addition, Smart Cookies are calorie-reduced. How do they compare with other cookies in the calorie department? Consider the following: oatmeal cookies made from a recipe in a popular cookbook provide about 125 calories each when they include chocolate chips; 110 calories without the chips (and most of these calories are empty). The comparable Smart Cookies, High-Flying Oatmeal Kites, contain just 50 hard-working calories each (none of them empty).

Honey spice cookies made from a recipe in a well-known women's magazine provide 180 calories each. A similar Smart Cookie, Mixed-Grain Peanut Almond Squares (made with honey and spices), provide only 70 calories.

Smart Cookies for babies, teens, and athletes have slightly higher calorie counts because of the increased energy requirements of these groups. But no cookies anywhere have more health-building nutrients.

Smart Cookies are for *everyone*. In addition to lunchbox and after-school goodies, and special ideas for your collegian's next survival package, you'll find wholesome morsels created for women "eating for two"; confections just right for your next dinner party or romantic tête-à-tête; snacks with magical energy-boosting ingredients perfect for marathon runners, aerobic dancers, parents chasing after small children, and executives struggling with the stress that comes with success; and much more. And although each chapter contains cookies that have been created to meet the needs of a different age group or activity, everyone will find tempting treats to enjoy on every page.

The cookies in this book accentuate the positive, eliminate the negatives, and multiply your chances of enjoying good health at every stage of life. And best of all, with these family-tested recipes, you'll find that in the pursuit of health and vigor, your taste buds never had it so good! As one nibbler put it at a lecture I gave recently, "All this, and heaven, too." Smart Cookies may pack a nutritional wallop, but their delectable flavors will make your tongue dance a jig.

Anyone who still doubts the taste excitement of wholesome food will swallow his skepticism with the first bite of a Smart Cookie. So turn the page, and get set to enjoy some smart snacking.

COOKIE SHELF
INGREDIENTS

FLOURS, GRAINS, AND SEEDS

Whole Wheat Flour

Regular whole wheat flour used in bread-making is made from hard winter wheat and contains a high degree of gluten, which helps the dough to rise. Whole wheat pastry flour, the kind recommended for most of these recipes, is made from soft spring wheat, has less gluten, and makes cookies of a finer texture. Both kinds of flour are rich in nutrients essential to the assembly line that keeps your body running on all cylinders.

Wheat Germ

There are some foods which, when used liberally, provide you with a broad spectrum of almost all the vitamins, minerals, and enzymes you need to keep that wonderful machine of yours in tip-top shape. It's unfortunate that one of these foods should have an unattractive name—making it sound like something that creeps! In this instance, however, the word "germ" means heart or essence of life; wheat germ is rich in life-giving nutrients that made bread the staff of life before flour was refined.

Unless you are using whole wheat flour, the wheat germ has been removed from the flour in your canister. It's been removed from most commercial baked goods—bread, cakes, crackers, noodles, and cookies. Why? Because wheat germ supports life; it attracts life-seeking insects and spoils more readily. Without the life-enhancing wheat germ, flour has a longer shelf life and can be shipped all over the world. It is therefore commercially expedient to remove the wheat germ from the flour.

What about enriched flour? That word "enriched" has been pulling the wool over our eyes and leading us down the path to deficiency diseases for too many years.

In the so-called "enrichment" process, only three or four of the thirty-three nutrients in wheat germ are put back in the flour, in only one-third of the original amount, and in a synthetic form which your body does not use effectively. Inorganic iron, for example, interferes with the body's use of vitamin E.

Wheat germ provides a bonanza of nutrients: lots of protein to repair and build cells, tissues, and organs; polyunsaturated oil for glowing complexions and efficient metabolism; vitamin E to protect polyunsaturates from oxidation, thus retarding the aging process and damage to the circulatory system; and practically every member of the B-complex family, in generous amounts. These vitamins are crucial to maintaining a healthy heart, an upbeat attitude, and a clear-thinking mind. Some of the B vitamins have been shown to improve the developing intelligence of young children.

Wheat germ also provides a veritable gold mine of minerals—magnesium, potassium, and calcium, essential to every beat of the heart; and zinc, so important to growth in children, to one's senses of taste and smell, to the ability to heal, to a blemish-free complexion, and to fertility and the health of the prostate gland.

Either toasted or raw wheat germ can be used in these recipes. Raw wheat germ has slightly more nutritional value; the toasted has better keeping qualities and a flavor more acceptable to some palates. I suggest using raw wheat germ in recipes that require baking and toasted wheat germ in unbaked confections.

Keep wheat germ in the refrigerator, or, better yet, in the freezer. It can be used directly from the freezer and will stay fresh longer. Never use rancid wheat germ. If you have a jar that's been around

7

for more than a month, give it the sniff-and-taste test. If it has an off odor or leaves a bitter after-taste, discard it and get a fresh supply.

Soy Flour

Soy flour is made from ground soy beans. It is very high in protein (about 40 percent), and remarkably high in potassium (one cup contains 1,636 milligrams). It is available with varying degrees of the original fat left in, as full fat, low fat, and defatted. Since the fat is a good source of lecithin, a substance that emulsifies cholesterol, I use the full-fat variety. It has a strong, almost bitter flavor, and should therefore be used sparingly. Since its amino acids complement those in wheat, you need only two tablespoons of soy flour at the bottom of a cup of wheat flour to greatly enhance the protein value of your Smart Cookies.

Soy grits and soy flakes are also used in some Smart Cookies. Soy grits are coarsely ground soy beans, not subjected to heat, and soy flakes are derived from lightly toasted beans that have been flaked. They have the nutritional qualities of soy beans but cook up much faster.

Rice Flour

Rice flour is made from ground brown rice, and can be used measure for measure as a substitute for wheat flour for those who cannot tolerate wheat. It is a good source of iron, the B vitamins, and protein, and is very low in sodium.

Rice polish (also known as rice bran) is ground from the outer coating of the rice grain. It is an excellent source of the B vitamin niacin. It also contains fiber, protein, minerals, and practically no sodium. It too has a slightly bitter taste, so use it sparingly.

Popcorn Flour

Popcorn flour is made from popped corn, with no fat added. A little more than one cup of popped corn ground in your food processor, blender, or seed mill will provide one cup of popcorn flour—and it contains only 50 calories. This type of flour will give the recipe a pleasant corn flavor.

Oats

Rolled oats is simply another name for ordinary, commercially available cereal oats or oatmeal (the "old-fashioned" kind, not the quick-cooking). Oats are a good source of B vitamins, calcium, potassium, and protein, and contain little sodium. They give Smart Cookies a hearty flavor and a chewy consistency.

Hi-Lysine Cornmeal

Hi-lysine cornmeal is derived from a recently developed breed of corn containing high levels of amino acids, especially lysine and tryptophan, essential factors that are usually found in small amounts in grains. Besides containing the necessary amino acids in the proportions in which the body uses them, Hi-lysine is superior to other cornmeals in that it is organically grown and made from the entire kernel, including the hull for extra fiber. It is available at some health-food stores or from E and D Grain Co., Fullerton, Nebraska 68638.

Millet

A major staple grain in Africa, millet is so rich in minerals that, unlike other grains, it is alkaline-forming rather than acid-forming. It provides protein and some B vitamins, notably B1 or thiamine, known as the "morale vitamin."

Bran

Coarse miller's bran is an excellent source of fiber, which has been shown to prevent many digestive and colon problems. It has a bland flavor which is not detectable in your Smart Cookies, but its dryness causes thirst—and this may encourage the children to drink more milk or juice. Like wheat germ, it should be kept refrigerated.

Amaranth

This ancient food of the Aztecs is now available in many natural foods stores. It has many of the cooking properties of grains, but because it is a plant food, not a grain, it can be tolerated by those who are allergic to the wheat family.

Seeds

"To stay young and vital all the days of your life," a physician once told me, "eat each day something which, if put into the ground, would grow." What did you eat today which, if put into the ground, would grow? Give up? How about seeds—sunflower, pumpkin, sesame, poppy.

When you stop to think about it, the seed is the very core of life. Its tiny kernel contains a mysterious and fantastic concentration of energy and nutrients designed by Nature, the master chemist, to get the plant up and keep it growing. This core of life in seeds bring vitality to those who consume them.

Consider the powerhouse of nutrients you get in seeds. They are a remarkable, unspoiled source of unsaturated fatty acids. Sunflower seeds are especially high in precious linoleic acid, which helps to prevent harmful deposits of cholesterol and improves resistance to disease by strengthening connective tissue in the cells.

Seeds are rich in vitamin E, which helps maintain normal viscosity in the blood, thus lessening the risk of life-threatening blood clots.

Seeds are a rich source of the B vitamins, containing more than you get in an equivalent quantity of wheat germ.

They are an excellent source of minerals, including the important trace minerals. The sunflower feeds voraciously on minerals. Its roots go down deep to draw up trace minerals not ordinarily present in topsoil, such as fluorine, which is essential for tooth enamel.

One of the most valuable contributions of seeds is their store of enzymes, which initiate and fulfill all vital processes in the cells. Enzymes are as fragile as they are vital, and cooking destroys many of them. Therefore, many of the Smart Cookies containing seeds are not exposed to heat, so you can reap full value from their storehouse of life-enhancing nutrients.

A seed mill is a very useful piece of equipment for grinding seeds into meal. It can also be used to grind nuts and pulverize dried orange and lemon peel into powdered rind. It handles small quantities very efficiently. You'll find them at specialty shops and in some health-food stores. A coffee grinder can be used instead, if you prefer.

SWEETENERS

The sweeteners used in most commercial cookies are refined sugar, either white or brown (white sugar with a little molasses added for color), and corn syrup, which is also highly refined and depleted of nutrients. These refined sweeteners make a mad rush for the bloodstream without paying a courtesy call on the liver, whose job it is to dole out the sugar in usable amounts. An abundance of sugar in the bloodstream triggers an over-production of insulin, which transports the sugar out of the blood and into the cells of the body, where it is converted into fat (making it very hard to zip your jeans).

In its eagerness to do its job, insulin overreacts and reduces the blood sugar to dangerously low levels. This causes hypoglycemia (low blood sugar), a condition that can masquerade as mental disorders, fatigue, temper tantrums, or erratic behavior. We agonize over "what's eating the kids" when they are irritable. Perhaps it's time to start wondering what the kids have been eating!

A recent landmark study conducted at the Tidewater Detention Homes in Tidewater, Virginia, revealed that by revising the diets of 276 juveniles, antisocial behavior declined by 44 percent, there were 77 percent fewer incidents of theft, 82 percent fewer incidents of assault, and a 55 percent reduction in the refusal to obey orders. What brought about this remarkable improvement in deportment? The amount of sugar in the young people's diets had been considerably reduced.

There is no refined sugar or corn syrup in *Smart Cookies.* Indeed, all sweetening agents have been reduced to a bare minimum because no sweetener should be used in excessive amounts. You'll be able to detect the lovely natural sweetness that is present in all wholesome food.

The following sweeteners contain some vitamins, minerals, and enzymes, which means they do not rush to your bloodstream and do not deplete your body's supply of vitamins in order to be metabolized.

Fruit Juice Concentrates

Fruit juice concentrates are incredibly sweet and rich in nutrients, and can be substituted for or used in conjunction with other sweeteners. Since the fruits they are made from may differ in sweetness, I suggest you give your batter the taste test. You may need a little more of another sweetener for the most appealing flavor.

Honey

This ingredient should be raw and unprocessed. Clover honey is the mildest and is recommended while you are weaning the family away from white sugar. Once they are accustomed to the taste, experiment with more exotic varieties, such as buckwheat, wildflower, and orange blossom.

Maple Syrup

Maple syrup contains 65 percent sucrose, as opposed to sugar cane and turbinado sugar, each of which contains 99 percent or more. Brown sugar is about 96 percent sucrose. Sucrose is the culprit that triggers the "sugar blues," or fluctuations in blood sugar levels.

Maple Syrup Granules

Maple syrup granules are a dry, all-natural sweetener made from pure maple syrup. In the conversion from syrup to powder, nothing is added and nothing is removed except water. It needs no refrigeration and will not ferment. The granules, tiny beige pellets, can be reconstituted by adding boiling water or can be used as a dry sweetener to replace cane sugar. Rich in calcium, they have much less sodium than honey.

Molasses

Unsulphured molasses is made from the juice of sugar cane. One tablespoon of first extraction or light molasses provides 33 milligrams of calcium, 183 milligrams of potassium, and almost 1 milligram of iron.

One tablespoon of second extraction or medium molasses provides 137 milligrams of calcium (as much as half a glass of milk), 213 milligrams of potassium, and 1.2 milligrams of iron.

One tablespoon of third extraction or blackstrap molasses provides 137 milligrams of calcium, 585 milligrams of potassium (more than you get in two oranges), and 3.2 milligrams of iron (that's ten times as much iron as you would get in a tablespoon of raisins), and only 43 calories. For that same 43 calories, you also get an extra bonus of magnesium, zinc, copper, chromium, and small amounts of thiamine, riboflavin, and niacin.

The flavor of blackstrap is strong and pervasive, and it has only half the sweetening power of sugar. For best results, it's a good idea to use honey or some other sweetener in conjunction with grain sweeteners and molasses, so that one flavor does not predominate.

Barley Malt Syrup

Barley malt syrup is a grain sweetener made from malted or germinated barley. It is 65 percent maltose and has much less sweetening power than sugar or honey, but since it does not need insulin for metabolizing, it does not trigger fluctuations in blood sugar levels.

Rice and Sorghum Syrups

Rice and sorghum syrups are also derived from grains and can be used to increase both moistness and the keeping quality of your cookies. Sorghum tastes very much like molasses.

FATS

Polyunsaturates

Safflower, sunflower, sesame, soy, and corn are polyunsaturated oils providing essential fatty acids, important building blocks for every cell in the body. They are called essential because the body cannot manufacture them—they must be consumed. Polyunsaturates have the added function of lowering cholesterol levels. They are, however, chemically very reactive, meaning they are converted by oxygen into peroxides, which break down into free radicals that damage the cells of the body.

Nature in her infinite wisdom packages these fatty acids with vitamin E, which prevents peroxidation. Processing frequently removes the vitamin E, so therefore it is important to supplement your diet of polyunsaturated oils with vitamin E.

Mono-Unsaturates

Olive oil, peanut oil, and chicken fat are mono-unsaturates. For some time it was thought that these fats were neutral—that they neither raised nor lowered cholesterol. But a recent study by Dr. Fred Mattson of the University of California at San Diego reveals that the mono-unsaturates, like polyunsaturates, are cholesterol reducers.

The American Heart Association and the National Cancer Institute both recommend a diet containing no more than 30 percent of calories from fat, with equal amounts of all three types: 10 percent polyunsaturates, 10 percent mono-unsaturates, and 10 percent saturated fats (butter, beef fat, coconut oil, and palm oil).

Butter

Pure unsalted, sweet butter is the kind that goes into Smart Cookies—but the amount is greatly reduced from most cookie recipes. In small amounts, butter provides so much salivary pleasure that its benefits exceed its risks.

Do not be tempted to substitute margarine for butter. There is no comparison in taste and healthwise you're much better off with butter. The hydrogenation process converts the polyunsaturated fatty acids into trans-fatty acids, which are more damaging to the arteries than saturated fats or cholesterol.

Butter has the same number of calories as margarine, and 20 percent fewer calories than oil.

Oil is 100 percent fat, while butter is 20 percent water and 80 percent fat. If you wish to substitute oil for butter, use 20 percent less oil. For example, if the recipe calls for one cup of butter, use 1 cup of oil minus 3 tablespoons, and add 3 tablespoons of liquid to the recipe. If the recipe does not call for any liquid, add 3 tablespoons of water or fruit juice with the oil.

OTHER INGREDIENTS

Carob

Carob, which is derived from the pod of the carob tree, is often used as a substitute for chocolate, and many people find the tastes identical. Unlike chocolate, however, carob contains natural sweeteners, and therefore requires fewer added sweeteners and is far less caloric. Three-and-a-half ounces of bittersweet chocolate contain 477 calories, 39.7 grams of fat, and 1.8 grams of fiber; the equivalent amount of carob contains 180 calories, 1.4 grams of fat, and a whopping 7.7 grams of roughage—which puts carob in the same league as wheat bran in the fiber department. Its carbohydrates are derived from fruit sugars, which have a low fat content—2% in carob compared to 52% in chocolate. The pectin content of carob has proved valuable in the treatment of diarrhea.

Lecithin

Lecithin is a fatty substance that acts as a natural emulsifier, and helps keep your blood's cholesterol circulating freely. Research indicates that lecithin increases by a factor of three the amount of cholesterol dissolved in bile salts, the vehicle by which the body rids itself of excess cholesterol. M.I.T. scientists have shown that lecithin in the diet improves memory and actually makes one "smarter." It does this by helping to manufacture acetylcholine, a substance that helps the brain to transmit nerve signals.

Nutritional or Brewer's Yeast

Nutritional yeast, also known as brewer's yeast, should not be confused with baker's yeast, which is used to raise dough. Brewer's yeast is a food supplement, a concentrated source of B vitamins, minerals, and high-quality protein—all this and no fat. Studies have shown that only one tablespoon of brewer's yeast a day can reduce cholesterol levels, raise glucose tolerance, and increase the ability to handle stress. Add a little to Smart Cookies, as well as to soups, stews, and muffins, and you'll easily down a tablespoon daily.

A note about where to find the products used in *Smart Cookies:* All the ingredients are available at many of the better supermarkets and practically all health-food stores. Among the mail-order sources for many of these items are: Shiloh Farms, Sulphur Springs, Arizona 72768; Walnut Acres, Penns Creek, Pennsylvania 17862; and Arrowhead Mills, Hereford, Texas 79045.

COOKIE CRAFT

The cookies in this book may be mixed by hand, blender, mixing machine, or food processor.

There are two basic types of cookies: those that are rolled out with a rolling pin, which should be thin and crisp; and those that are dropped from spoons, which are softer and contain more moisture than thin cookies.

If you should find yourself strapped for time to make individual drops, bake the dough in square or rectangular cake pans about 5 minutes longer than the directions call for, and then cut into squares. Thin cookie dough, also known as stiff dough, can also be shaped or cut out with special cookie cutters, as the occasion dictates—gingerbread people, Halloween witches, Thanksgiving pilgrims, Christmas Santas, Chanukah menorahs, and Valentine hearts. It can also be rolled, then sliced and baked, as for refrigerator cookies; shaped into balls; or pressed from a cookie press.

Most of the recipes in this book call for whole wheat pastry flour. Humidity and the size of the eggs (large eggs are recommended, but are not essential) affect the amount of flour needed. Too little flour means the cookies will spread; too much makes them tough.

To test for the right amount of flour, beat in almost all the flour required in the recipe. Touch the dough lightly with an unfloured finger. If your finger comes away sticky, add more flour—in small amounts to avoid excess.

To bake cookies, use cookie sheets rather than pans with sides, so the cookies can slide off. No sides also means better browning.

If you line your cookie sheets with parchment paper (found in gourmet cookware shops and some health-food stores), you will not need to grease or wash the pan. If you are not using parchment paper, try greasing the pan with a half teaspoon of liquid lecithin, combined with a half teaspoon oil.

Cookies will dry out if they bake too slowly, so place the oven rack on the top rung where browning is fastest, and be sure to preheat the oven.

Your cookies are finished when they are nicely browned. Wait a couple of minutes before you remove them with a wide spatula. Don't wait too long or they'll stick. If this should happen, return the pan to the oven for a minute.

Avoid storing crisp and soft cookies together. Crisp cookies will absorb moisture from the soft cookies and wilt. If crisp cookies have wilted, simply place them in a 300°F oven for 10 minutes.

Store a lemon, orange, or apple with soft cookies. The cookies will absorb the fruit's delicate flavor and remain soft.

Cookie dough wrapped in plastic wrap can be stored in the refrigerator for three months, or in the freezer for about six months. Baked cookies will keep about three weeks in the refrigerator and up to a year in the freezer.

1

SMART COOKIES
FOR WOMEN
WHO ARE EATING FOR TWO

Whether you are pregnant or nursing a child, now is not the time to diet. Never in your life is what you eat so vital to the life of another. This is the time to enjoy good food. As Tom Brewer, M.D., writes in *Metabolic Toxemia of Late Pregnancy: A Disease of Malnutrition*, ''Severe caloric restriction, which has been very commonly recommended, is potentially harmful to the developing fetus and to the mother. Mothers who gain an average of 36 pounds have babies with fewer abnormalites.''

A few words of caution: at all other times, we advise throwing away the salt shaker. *But not during pregnancy.* You should salt to taste, and with good conscience. Sodium contributes to water retention, which is a good thing during pregnancy. Sodium helps maintain the increased blood volume needed to nourish the baby.

When you are nursing, there will be a heavy drain on your calcium supply. The baby has priority in this department even if the calcium he needs must be extracted from your bones. A good breakfast is important. Chances are you won't have time to prepare and eat an elaborate breakfast before the clarion call from the nursery. It's a good idea to have some of these cookies handy for nibbling. They are rich in protein, iron, calcium, and the whole vitamin B family, all of which helps to put the glow of health on you and your baby.

Along with a good diet, the cookies I have devised for you can help you enjoy nine months of glowing expectations—and give you the energy to enjoy the first months after your baby is born.

Crispy Ginger Satellites

Fly high with these delicious ginger cookies that really spice up your day. According to a recent study (*Lancet*, March 20, 1982), ginger may help subdue the collywobbles, motion sickness, and queasiness that many women experience in the early months of pregnancy. The milk powder, molasses, and wheat germ provide much-needed calcium and B vitamins. B1 (thaimine) and B6 (pyridoxine) have also been shown to relieve the nausea of pregnancy.

¼ cup butter
¼ cup molasses or honey
1 egg
½ teaspoon baking soda
¼ teaspoon salt
1 tablespoon water
2 cups whole wheat pastry
    flour, minus 2 tablespoons

2 tablespoons wheat germ
2 tablespoons milk powder
1 tablespoon ground ginger
    sunflower seeds for garnish
    (about ¼ cup)

In food processor, blender, or mixing bowl, blend butter, molasses or honey, and egg until smooth. Combine the baking soda, salt, and water and stir into the liquid mixture. Add the flour, wheat germ, milk powder, and ginger, and blend only until incorporated and dough is stiff.

Preheat oven to 350°F.

Pinch off pieces of dough the size of walnuts, flatten between your hands, and place on cookie sheet lined with parchment paper or greased with a mixture of a few drops of liquid lecithin and oil. Top

each cookie with sunflower seeds. For variety, leave some of the cookies unpressed, in the shape of walnuts. Bake for about 12 minutes. To maintain their delicious crispness, store in airtight container.
Yield: 3 dozen.
Approximately 50 calories each.

Happy Delivery Carob-Walnut Clusters

A crunchy, nutty celebration treat, rich in strengthening nutrients, and deliciously reminiscent of that old-time sweet shop flavor.

- ¼ cup butter
- ¼ cup honey
- 1 egg
- 1½ teaspoons vanilla
- 5 tablespoons carob powder
- ¼ teaspoon salt
- ½ cup whole wheat pastry flour
- 1½ cups coarsely broken walnuts

In food processor, blender, or mixing bowl, combine butter, honey, egg, and vanilla. Process or mix until smooth. Add the carob powder, salt, and flour. Mix until ingredients are well-combined, then stir in the walnuts.

Preheat oven to 325°F.

Drop the batter by teaspoonfuls onto a cookie sheet lined with parchment paper or greased with a mixture of a few drops of liquid lecithin and oil. Bake for 15 minutes.
Yield: 36 clusters.
Approximately 60 calories each.

Banana Pecan Tartlets

Bananas become incredibly sweet when they are frozen, making it unnecessary to add a concentrated sweetener. A delicious pick-me-up—something all mothers and mothers-to-be need!

1 cup mashed banana
⅓ cup sunflower seeds
3 tablespoons peanut butter
    (smooth or chunky)

1 teaspoon vanilla
½ teaspoon cinnamon
    pecans and carob chips for
    garnish

In food processor, blender, or mixing bowl, combine banana, sunflower seeds, peanut butter, vanilla, and cinnamon, and blend until ingredients are well-mixed.

Line the cups of a muffin pan with paper liners. Place one heaping tablespoon of the batter in each. Top some with pecans and, for variety, some with carob chips. Place in freezer. Remove from freezer a few minutes before serving.

Yield: 12 miniature tarts.

Approximately 60 calories each.

High-Calcium Granola Pepita Squares

These unbaked, easy-to-make confections are a powerhouse of nutrients needed by mother and child. Calcium is necessary not only for bone and teeth formation, but also for blood clotting and for the nerves. Pumpkin seeds are rich in zinc, which recent research points to as necessary to the baby's future learning ability.

1 cup peanut butter (smooth or chunky)
½ cup dry milk powder
½ cup honey or molasses
½ cup wheat germ

1 cup granola (recipe follows)
½ cup coconut
2 tablespoons pepitas (pumpkin seeds), lightly toasted (or substitute sunflower seeds)

In food processor, blender, or mixing bowl, combine peanut butter and honey or molasses. Add dry milk, wheat germ, granola, and coconut, and mix well. Spread the mixture in a 9 × 13-inch dish lined with parchment paper or greased with a mixture of a few drops of liquid lecithin and oil, and press pumpkin or sunflower seeds into the mixture. Cut into 1½-inch squares and refrigerate or freeze.
Yield: 4 dozen.
Approximately 60 calories each.

CRUNCHY RAISIN GRANOLA

This power-packed granola mix is sweet and crunchy though it has no added fat or sweeteners. Eat it for breakfast and use it in all recipes calling for granola.

½ cup raisins
1 cup hot water
3 cups uncooked rolled oats
1 cup unsweetened shredded
    coconut
½ cup sesame seeds
½ cup sunflower seeds

½ cup soy grits or flakes
¼ cup dry milk powder
1 teaspoon cinnamon
½ cup wheat germ
¼ cup bran
½ cup chopped or sliced
    almonds (optional)

Soak the raisins in the water overnight.

Preheat oven to 250°F.

In a large bowl, combine the oats, coconut, sesame and sunflower seeds, soy grits or flakes, dry milk, cinnamon, and almonds (if desired). Mix in the wheat germ and bran.

Pour the water off the soaked raisins into a cup. Pour this raisin liquid over the oat mixture and mix to moisten the grains. Add the soaked raisins. Spread the mixture on two cookie sheets lined with parchment paper or greased with a mixture of a few drops of liquid lecithin and oil. Bake for one hour, stirring the mixture every 15 minutes. When the granola cools, store in tightly lidded containers. Keep refrigerated or frozen.

Yield: 2 quarts.

Approximately 400 calories per cup.

Peanut and Raisin Cookies

The combination of wheat, soy, and cornmeal, with their complementary amino acids, enriches these biscuit-like cookies with high-
quality protein. The butters provide fat necessary to the development
of baby's brain; wheat germ and raisins are good sources of iron; and
the milk offers bone-building calcium. Keep some of these handy
while you sit nursing the baby, and nibble in good health.

2 eggs
½ cup milk
¼ cup unsalted (sweet) butter
1 teaspoon grated nutmeg
1 teaspoon vanilla
⅔ cup peanut butter (smooth
or chunky)
½ cup yellow cornmeal
(preferably Hi-lysine)

1 cup whole wheat pastry
flour, minus 2 tablespoons
2 tablespoons soy flour
1 teaspoon baking powder
¼ cup wheat germ
½ cup raisins
peanut halves or chunks for
garnish

In food processor, blender, or mixing bowl, combine eggs, milk,
butter, nutmeg, vanilla, and peanut butter. Blend until smooth.

In another bowl, combine the cornmeal, flours, baking powder,
and wheat germ. Process or mix until ingredients are combined.
Fold in raisins.

Preheat oven to 350°F.

Drop the batter by tablespoonfuls 2 inches apart on a cookie sheet
lined with parchment paper or greased with a mixture of a few drops

of liquid lecithin and oil. Garnish liberally with peanuts. Bake for 10 to 15 minutes or until deliciously browned.
Yield: 2 dozen.
Approximately 100 calories each.

Sesame Coconut Almond Cookies

Share these mouth-watering cookies with the love of your life. They are sky-high in potassium and rich in zinc, a trace mineral very important to growth, healing, and your sense of taste. And new research reveals that zinc is also important to the child's developing brain.

2 eggs
4 tablespoons butter
⅓ cup frozen orange juice
    concentrate, slightly thawed
2 tablespoons honey
½ teaspoon grated orange rind
½ teaspoon ginger
1 cup whole wheat pastry
    flour, minus 2 tablespoons
2 tablespoons soy flour
1 teaspoon baking powder

¼ cup wheat germ
¼ cup toasted almonds,
    chopped fine
2 tablespoons dry milk powder
½ cup unsweetened shredded
    coconut
½ cup dried currants or
    raisins (optional)
sesame seeds for garnish
    (approximately ¼ cup)

In food processor, blender, or mixing bowl, combine eggs, butter, orange juice, honey, and rind, and blend until smooth and creamy.

31

Add the ginger, flours, baking powder, wheat germ, almonds, milk powder, and coconut. Blend just until ingredients are well-mixed. Fold in currants or raisins.

Preheat oven to 325°F.

Drop the batter by teaspoonfuls onto a baking sheet lined with parchment paper or greased with a mixture of a few drops of liquid lecithin and oil. Top each cookie with a liberal sprinkling of sesame seeds. Bake for about 25 minutes or until nicely browned.

Yield: 3 dozen.

Approximately 55 calories each.

Four-Grain Sunflower Cookies

These crisp, delicious cookies contain millet, one of the most well-balanced and least allergenic of all the grains, rich in protein, minerals, vitamins, and lecithin, which emulsifies cholesterol. Combined with the cornmeal, oats, and either wheat, rice, or amaranth flour, millet enhances the flavor and protein found in these very special cookies.

2 eggs
1/3 cup honey
1/4 cup vegetable oil (preferably olive)
3/4 cup buttermilk or yogurt
2 tablespoons frozen concentrated orange juice, slightly thawed
1 teaspoon vanilla
1/4 cup millet
1/4 cup cornmeal
1/4 cup rolled oats, ground to a flour
1 cup whole wheat, rice, or amaranth flour
sunflower seeds for garnish (approximately 1/4 cup)

In food processor, blender, or mixing bowl, combine eggs, honey, oil, buttermilk or yogurt, orange juice concentrate, and vanilla. Blend until smooth.

In another bowl, combine millet, cornmeal, oats, and flour. Add to egg mixture and process briefly till ingredients are combined.

Preheat oven to 300°F.

Drop dough from a tablespoon onto an ungreased cookie sheet. Top each cookie liberally with sunflower seeds. Bake for 30 minutes or until golden brown.

Yield: 3 dozen.

Approximately 40 calories each.

Chewy Apricot-Almond Granola Bars

Hippocrates must have been thinking of apricots and almonds when he said, "Let food be your medicine." A half cup of dried apricots provides 3½ milligrams of blood-building iron, some of the B vitamins, especially niacin, which is very important to maintain a pleasant dispositon, and a whopping 7,000 units of vitamin A, which helps you fight infection and which has recently been cited as an anti-cancer factor.

Almonds, too, are a nutritional miracle—an excellent source of protein (12 grams in a half cup), very rich in potassium, iron, calcium, and phosphorus, and high in essential polyunsaturated fatty acids, which tend to lower cholesterol levels. Apricots and almonds, plus the other wholesome ingredients in these confections, make them a wonderful afternoon pick-up.

While these are great for nursing mothers, the father of the baby can enjoy them too, as well as the baby's brothers and sisters. Take them along when you go shopping with your toddler—you'll be able to resist the junk food temptations during your trip.

1¼ cups rolled oats
½ cup sunflower seeds
1 egg, lightly beaten
2 tablespoons honey or
    molasses
½ cup peanut butter
    (smooth or chunky)
¼ cup wheat germ
2 tablespoons dry milk
    powder

½ teaspoon cinnamon
½ cup dried apricots,
    chopped
2 tablespoons raisins
    (optional)
½ cup almond slices, lightly
    toasted

Toast the oats and sunflower seeds on a cookie sheet in a 350°F oven for 5 to 7 minutes, or until dry and crisp.

In a saucepan over low heat, combine the lightly beaten egg, honey or molasses, and peanut butter. Stir with wooden spoon until ingredients are well-combined, then turn off heat.

Add the toasted oats and seeds, wheat germ, milk powder, cinnamon, apricots, and raisins.

Press the mixture into an 8-inch-square dish, lined with parchment paper or lightly oiled with a mixture of liquid lecithin and oil.

Press the toasted almonds over the top of the granola mixture. Cut into 1½-inch pieces and refrigerate or freeze.

Yield: 25 squares.

Approximately 65 calories each.

Carob Peanut Butter Bars

Crunchy sesame and sunflower seeds and creamy peanut butter merge with the chocolaty flavor of carob to form a sensational snack rich in vitamins and minerals, and very high in the potassium necessary to the smooth functioning of your heart, and your baby's.

¼ cup honey
2 tablespoons blackstrap molasses
1 teaspoon vanilla
½ cup peanut butter (smooth or chunky)
½ cup carob powder
½ cup sunflower seeds
½ cup sesame seeds

¼ cup wheat germ
½ teaspoon cinnamon
1 to 2 tablespoons water or orange juice (enough to achieve a smooth consistency)
unsweetened shredded coconut or chopped walnuts for garnish

In a medium-sized bowl, combine honey, molasses, vanilla, and peanut butter. Mix with wooden spoon until ingredients are combined.

Add the carob powder, seeds, wheat germ, and cinnamon, and mix. If mixture is dry, blend in the water or juice.

Spread the batter in an 8-inch-square ungreased dish. Press coconut or nuts over the surface. Cut into 1½-inch squares and refrigerate or freeze.

Yield: 25 squares.
Approximately 90 calories each.

Feeling Good Wheat Sprout Bonbons

Sprouting the wheat grains creates an explosion of nutrients, especially the B vitamins, and causes the development of vitamin C even though there is no vitamin C in the dry grains. Raisins contribute iron, so necessary for the hemoglobin that transports life-giving oxygen to the cells of mother and babe. Nuts and seeds provide protein, many essential minerals, and the important unsaturated fatty acids.

1 cup wheat sprouts
    (instructions follow)
½ cup pecans
½ cup sunflower seeds
1 cup raisins
1 tablespoon honey, molasses,
    or malt syrup

½ teaspoon cinnamon
¼ teaspoon salt
    unsweetened coconut shreds
    (about ¼ cup)

Combine sprouts, nuts, seeds, and raisins in food processor or blender. Add honey, cinnamon, and salt, and mix well. Form into 1-inch balls and roll in coconut.
Yield: 2 dozen.
Approximately 55 calories each.

TO GROW WHEAT SPROUTS

Put 3 tablespoons of wheat grains (available at natural-food stores) in a pint jar. Give them a quick rinse to remove surface dirt, then fill the jar halfway with tepid water. Cover and let stand overnight. Next morning, cover the jar with two layers of cheesecloth secured with a rubber band, or with a screened lid that can be purchased at gourmet shops and natural-food stores. (You can also make your own screened lid from window screen cut to fit a jar ring.)

Without removing the screened lid, pour off the water into a glass. Do not discard the water—it has valuable vitamins and minerals and can be added to soups or used to cook potatoes or rice, or to steam vegetables.

Next, rinse the grains with tepid water, pour off the rinse water (give it to your plants), and let the jar rest under the sink or on the sink, slightly tilted so excess moisture can drain off. Use a sponge or folded dishcloth to prop up the jar bottom. Cover the jar with a tea towel—the grains germinate best in the dark (modesty, I suppose).

Repeat the rinsing procedure 2 or 3 times throughout the next two days. By the end of the second day, your wheat sprouts will be ready. Refrigerate them if you're not using them immediately.

Follow the same procedure for other grains, like triticale and rye, and for garbanzo beans (also known as chick-peas).

2

SMART COOKIES
FOR TEETHING BABIES,
TODDLERS, AND PRESCHOOLERS

Children need to eat many of the foods their parents are cutting down on. So don't put the children on your diet!

You are very wisely limiting your calories and cutting down on fats, but bear in mind that babies and preschoolers need substantial amounts of fats and cholesterol to ensure the full development of their intellectual powers.

Eggs are one of the brain foods recommended by Ralph E. Minear, M.D., author of *The Brain Food Diet for Children*. Not only are eggs a good source of dietary fat, they are rich in lecithin, which, as I've mentioned, produces acetylcholine, one of the chemicals that acts as a transmitter for brain impulses within the body. Children need all kinds of fats, saturated, unsaturated, and cholesterol, Dr. Minear maintains. They are key elements in any diet that centers on brain development.

Children also need vitamins, minerals, and complex carbohydrates, all of which are provided in the Smart Cookies we have devised for your smart cookie.

Cookies to Cut Your Teeth On

Rich in calcium and iron, these cookies help to build strong teeth while they comfort sore gums. Your baby will chomp happily and in good health.

1 egg yolk, beaten
2 tablespoons blackstrap
   molasses
2 tablespoons vegetable oil
1 teaspoon vanilla extract

¾ cup whole wheat pastry
   flour
1 tablespoon soy flour
1 tablespoon wheat germ
1 tablespoon dry milk powder

In food processor, blender, or mixing bowl, blend the egg yolk, molasses, oil, and vanilla.

Preheat oven to 350°F.

Combine the flours, wheat germ, and milk powder, and add them to the egg mixture to make a dough. Roll the dough out on a lightly floured surface. Place the dough on a cookie sheet lined with parchment paper or greased lightly with a mixture of liquid lecithin and oil. Cut the dough into rectangles no bigger than a baby's finger.

Bake for 8 to 10 minutes. Cool on a wire rack.

Yield: 3 dozen.

Approximately 20 calories each.

Teddy Bear Treats

Give your toddlers a dish of grated carrots, raisins, seeds, and nuts and let them decorate their very own teddy bear cookies. If they eat some in the process, so who's counting?

½ cup vegetable oil
¼ cup honey
1 teaspoon vanilla
¼ cup orange or apple juice
½ teaspoon ginger
1 teaspoon cinnamon
2 cups whole wheat pastry
   flour

¼ cup soy flour
2 tablespoons wheat germ
   raisins, currants, poppy
      seeds, apple butter, and
      nuts for decoration

In food processor, blender, or mixing bowl, combine oil, honey, vanilla, and juice. Blend until smooth and creamy.

Combine ginger, cinnamon, flours, and wheat germ, and add to the liquid mixture until it forms a dough. Divide dough into 4 pieces and wrap each in wax paper or plastic wrap. Refrigerate for an hour.

Preheat oven to 350°F.

Roll out each piece of the dough to a ¼-inch thickness. Cut each with a large round cookie cutter; you should be able to make two 3-inch circles out of each piece of dough, with some left over, which we will soon put to work.

Place four of the circles at the top of a cookie sheet lined with parchment paper or greased with a mixture of a few drops of liquid lecithin and oil. Using a finger, make two indentations in each of the circles to form wide eyes. Place a dab of the apple butter in each. Add little bits of the leftover dough to the sides of the four circles to form ears. (Moisten the joints with a little water to more effectively attach the body parts.)

Attach the remaining four circles underneath the heads to form pudgy bodies. If you are feeling creative, make fat arms and legs with leftover dough. Use raisins, currants, poppy seeds, or nuts for additional trimming.

Bake for 10 to 15 minutes. Let them cool for a minute, then remove to a wire rack.

Yield: 4 large bears.

Approximately 500 calories in each bear—about 10 calories a nibble.

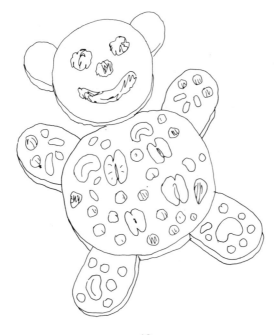

Molasses Peanut Butter Alphabet Letters

The children will be eating their words and loving every bite of these delicious morsels, which provide wholesome nutrients while introducing them to the alphabet in a most delightful way.

1 egg	*⅓ cup carob powder*
⅓ cup blackstrap molasses	*1 cup whole wheat pastry*
½ cup peanut butter (smooth	*flour, minus 2 tablespoons*
or chunky)	*2 tablespoons soy flour*
1 teaspoon vanilla	*sesame seeds (about ¼ cup)*

In food processor, blender, or mixing bowl, combine egg, molasses, peanut butter, and vanilla. Process or mix until ingredients are well-blended. Combine the carob and flours in a separate bowl and add to the egg mixture. The mixture will be the consistency of dough.

Divide the dough in 4 pieces, wrap in plastic wrap or waxed paper, and refrigerate for at least one hour.

Preheat oven to 325°F.

Grease two cookie sheets with a mixture of liquid lecithin and oil, or line them with parchment paper. Remove one portion of dough from the refrigerator and cut it into 12 pieces. Roll each piece into a 6-inch rope, and roll each rope in sesame seeds. Place them one at a time on the cookie sheets and twist them into different letters. Repeat with the rest of the dough, but save some dough to make the letters of your child's name. Bake for 8 to 10 minutes.

Yield: 4 dozen letters.

Approximately 35 calories each.

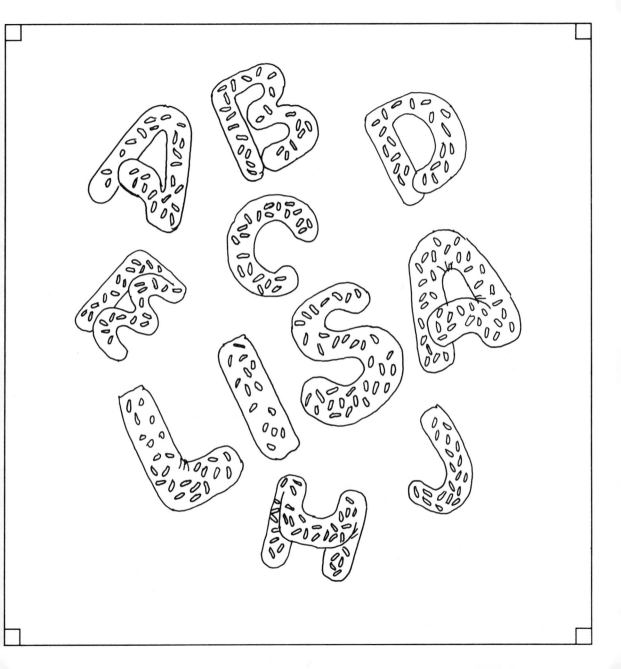

Rice Pudding Cookies

As dessert or as a special treat, these cookies fit the bill. Take some along on a shopping trip and share them with your toddler. They're rich in those great B vitamins that put a nice glow on your disposition—and on baby's.

1 egg
¼ cup butter, softened
¼ cup frozen apple or orange
    juice concentrate, slightly
    thawed
2 tablespoons molasses, maple
    syrup, or barley malt syrup
2 teaspoons vanilla
1 cup cooked brown rice
1 cup whole wheat pastry
    flour, minus 2 tablespoons

2 tablespoons soy flour
1 teaspoon baking soda
3 tablespoons wheat germ
1 teaspoon cinnamon
¼ teaspoon freshly grated or
    powdered nutmeg
½ cup currants or raisins
    carob chips and coconut for
    garnish

In food processor, blender, or mixing bowl, combine egg, butter, fruit juice, sweetener, vanilla, and rice. Mix until well-blended.

In another bowl, combine the flours, baking soda, wheat germ, cinnamon, and nutmeg. Mix briefly to combine ingredients. Fold in the currants or raisins.

Preheat oven to 350°F.

Drop the batter by teaspoonfuls onto a cookie sheet lined with parchment paper or greased with a mixture of liquid lecithin and oil. Press down with a wet fork. The thinner the dough, the crisper the cookies will be. Garnish each with a few carob chips and some coconut. Bake in upper third of oven for 12 to 15 minutes.

Yield: 4 dozen.

Approximately 50 calories each.

Butterfly Ginger Cookies

Let the kids draw pretty shapes onto the wings of these butterfly-shaped cookies with a delicious cream cheese icing flavored with orange.

⅓ cup vegetable oil
½ cup blackstrap molasses
3 cups whole wheat pastry
    flour
¼ cup soy flour
1 teaspoon baking soda

½ teaspoon cinnamon
½ teaspoon ginger
⅓ teaspoon cloves
¼ cup orange juice or water
    currants

CREAM CHEESE ICING

4 ounces of cream cheese
2 tablespoons frozen orange
    juice concentrate,
    slightly thawed

In food processor, blender, or mixing bowl, combine oil and molasses and blend until light and smooth. In another bowl, combine flours, baking soda, cinnamon, ginger, and cloves, and add to the molasses mixture. Blend. Add orange juice or water as needed to make a pliable dough. Chill about one hour.

Preheat oven to 350°F.

Draw a butterfly outline about 4 inches long onto cardboard with your child's assistance. Cut it out and grease one side of it. Roll half the dough at a time to ¼-inch thickness. Lay the butterfly pattern

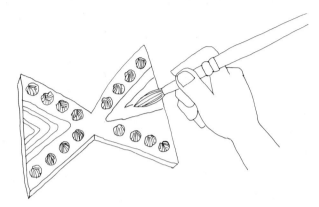

greased side down on the dough and cut around it with a sharp knife. Using a broad spatula, lift the dough onto a baking sheet lightly greased with a mixture of liquid lecithin and oil. Repeat procedure, or for variety, cut out other patterns. Store-bought cookie cutters can also be used.

Bake in the upper third of the oven for 12 minutes or until cookies spring back when gently tapped in the middle. Take them from oven before they brown and let them cool a few minutes before removing them to a wire rack.

Blend the cream cheese and orange juice concentrate until smooth. When the cookies are cold, decorate the butterflies using currants and the cream cheese frosting, which can be applied with a slim paint brush.

Yield: 20 butterflies.

Approximately 115 calories each.

3

SMART COOKIES
THAT GO TO SCHOOL
IN POCKET OR LUNCHBOX

These top-of-the-class nutty nuggets work two ways to help your child make the grade at school and cope with the difficult pre-adolescent years. First, they eliminate the negatives—the over-sweetened, oversalted, over-processed foods that lead to cavity corners, climb-the-wall hyperactivity, and muddle-headed mentality. Second, these cookies are rich in the nutrients necessary for health, vitality, and creative thinking skills.

These wholesome cookies may not make your child a genius, but they sure will help him or her fulfill his or her greatest potential.

To facilitate the preparation of these special confections, I suggest you keep on hand a supply of my special Dynamite Mix, a basic dough that is used for many of the recipes in this book (you'll see it in the lists of ingredients).

DYNAMITE MIX

1 cup sunflower seed meal
    (grind sunflower seeds
    in a seed mill or coffee
    grinder)
1 cup wheat germ
1 cup oat flour (process rolled
    oats in a blender)

1 cup corn meal (preferably
    Hi-lysine)
1 cup soy flour
½ cup dry milk powder
½ cup brewer's yeast
1 cup rice flour

Combine ingredients and store in the freezer, in a jar or plastic bag. Since many recipes in this book call for one cup of this mix, it would facilitate preparation if you stored one cup to one bag.

Any one of these ingredients may be omitted if you don't have it on hand or have an allergy to it. There are approximately 420 calories in one cup of Dynamite Mix.

School-Days Breakfast Bars

A good breakfast will keep your child's blood sugar levels on an even keel so they don't lag in the middle of the morning. These scrumptuous chewy granola bars can be eaten with your breakfast or, when you are rushed, instead of breakfast. They're rich in protein, complex carbohydrates, vitamins, and minerals. And take some along for lunch to prevent mid-afternoon slump.

1 egg
1 teaspoon vanilla
½ cup peanut butter
⅓ cup molasses or honey
2½ cups toasted oats (toast on cookie sheet for 15 minutes in 350°F oven)

1 cup Dynamite Mix (page 50)
1 teaspoon cinnamon or grated orange peel
1 cup raisins
1 cup chopped nuts

In food processor, blender, or mixing bowl, combine egg, vanilla, peanut butter, and molasses or honey, and process till well-mixed. In another bowl, combine the oats, Dynamite Mix, and cinnamon or orange peel, and process until ingredients are mixed. Add raisins and nuts.

Preheat oven to 350°F.

Press the mixture firmly into a 10 × 15-inch jelly-roll pan, well greased with a mixture of liquid lecithin and oil, or lined with parchment paper. Bake for 20 minutes. Cool slightly, then cut into 2-inch bars. Store in a tightly covered container in the freezer.

Yield: 40 bars.

Approximately 85 calories each.

Outer Space Saucers

They're out of this world—and chock-full of get-up-and-go nutrients. I can't make enough of them when my grandchildren are around. They're also great to make along with your children, because there is no baking involved. You can eat these right from the freezer or take them along. This cookie is a candy you can feel good about.

1 cup peanut butter (smooth or chunky)	¼ cup carob powder
	1 cup raisins
⅓ cup honey	1½ cups granola (page 29)

In a medium-sized bowl, combine peanut butter and honey, mixing with a wooden spoon. Mix in the carob powder, then fold in the raisins and granola. It will make a fairly stiff dough. Take handfuls of the dough and roll each on waxed paper into the shape of fat cigars. Place the cigars in the freezer.

When they are hard but not yet frozen solid, slice the cigars into nickel-sized pieces. If the cigars should get frozen, simply leave them at room temperature for a few minutes until they are thawed enough to slice.

Yield: about 8 cigars and a zillion "saucers."
Approximately 350 calories in each cigar.

Zucchini-Spice Mystery Bars

The wheat germ in these chewy delights provides vitamin E, which is thought to improve deductive reasoning. They are also rich in the mineral zinc, which helps you think more clearly.

2 cups whole wheat pastry
    flour, minus 2 tablespoons
½ cup wheat germ
½ cup rolled oats
1 teaspoon baking powder
1½ teaspoons baking soda
1 teaspoon ground cloves
1 teaspoon cinnamon
½ teaspoon ground nutmeg
¼ cup butter, cut in small
    pieces
⅓ cup honey

2 eggs
2 teaspoons vanilla
2 cups grated zucchini,
    unpeeled
¾ cup raisins or currants
½ cup chopped pecans,
    peanuts, or pumpkin
    seeds
carob chips, dried fruits,
    and nuts for the
    mystery ingredients

In a mixing bowl, combine the flour, wheat germ, oats, baking powder, baking soda, cloves, cinnamon, and nutmeg.

In food processor using the steel blade, in a blender, or in a mixing bowl, cream the butter and honey. Add the eggs, vanilla, and zucchini, and mix until well-blended. Add the combined dry ingredients and process briefly until all ingredients are integrated. Stir in the raisins and nuts.

Preheat oven to 325°F.

Drop the batter by teaspoonfuls onto a cookie sheet lined with parchment paper or greased with a few drops of liquid lecithin and oil.

Tuck a carob chip or two into some cookies. Tuck a banana chip into others. Tuck a slice of an Outer Space Saucer (page 52), half of a dried apricot, a whole almond, pecan, or filbert, or a couple of raisins into the remaining cookies. These are the mystery ingredients because they are hidden in the dough.

Bake for about 12 to 15 minutes. Leave cookies on cookie sheet for a few minutes, then remove to a wire rack to cool.

Yield: 6 dozen.

Approximately 35 calories each.

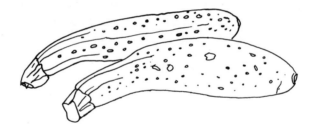

Big Banana Bozos

These nutty crunchies are fortified with brewer's yeast for extra protein to rev up your motor, and blackstrap molasses for blood-enriching iron.

⅔ cup whole wheat pastry
    flour
2 tablespoons soy flour
2 tablespoons wheat germ
2 tablespoons brewer's yeast
⅓ cup dry milk powder
1 teaspoon cinnamon
½ teaspoon powdered ginger
½ teaspoon nutmeg
½ cup chopped cashews,
    lightly roasted
½ cup sunflower seeds, lightly
    roasted

¼ cup vegetable oil
3 tablespoons blackstrap
    molasses
2 tablespoons honey
1 egg
1 large banana, mashed
    (about 1 cup)
½ cup raisins, or unsweetened
    carob chips, or some of
    each
    peanuts or carob chips for
    garnish

In a bowl, mix together the flours, wheat germ, yeast, milk powder, cinnamon, ginger, and nutmeg. Set aside.

In food processor, blender, or mixing bowl, combine oil, molasses, honey, egg, and mashed banana, and mix until light and fluffy. Add the dry ingredients and process until combined. Stir in the nuts, seeds, and carob chips or raisins.

Preheat oven to 325°F.

Drop the batter by tablespoonfuls onto two cookie sheets lined with parchment paper or greased with a few drops of liquid lecithin and oil. Top each cookie with several peanut halves or carob chips. Bake for 12 to 15 minutes or until firm. Transfer cookies to wire rack to cool.

Yield: 3 dozen.

Approximately 80 calories each.

Butter Pecan Touchdowns

Take some to the game and you'll be sure to score!

¼ cup unsalted (sweet) butter,
    cut in slices
¼ cup honey

or 1¼ cups Dynamite Mix (page 50)
{
1 cup whole wheat pastry
    flour
2 tablespoons wheat germ
2 tablespoons dry milk powder
}

½ cup chopped pecans
1 cup chopped dates or figs,
    or a mixture of the two
½ cup orange or apple juice
½ cup unsweetened shredded
    coconut, lightly toasted

Cook the dried fruit in the fruit juice until thick (about 15 minutes) or, if you have time, simply soak the fruit in the juice overnight.

Preheat oven to 375°F.

In food processor using the steel blade, or in blender or mixing bowl, cream together the butter and honey. Add flour, wheat germ, and dry milk, and process only until these are incorporated into the mixture. Stir in the pecans.

Spread the mixture in an ungreased pie plate as thin as possible, using a spatula. Bake for 15 minutes, then break it up into large crumbs and bake for 5 minutes longer until golden brown and crisp.

Let cool, then combine with the toasted coconut. Puree or mash the dried fruit mixture and combine it with the crunchy mixture. Roll the mixture into a cylinder about 2 inches in diameter. Roll in chopped pecans. Press the roll into an oval shape and refrigerate for several hours or overnight. Slice into ¼-inch football-shaped cookies.
Yield: about 2½ dozen.
Approximately 75 calories each.

High-Flying Oatmeal Kites

Full of crunchy goodies that make you feel you're on top of the world.

¼ cup unsalted (sweet) butter, cut in slices	½ cup whole wheat pastry flour
¼ cup honey	¼ cup wheat germ
⅓ cup peanut butter, smooth or chunky, or tahini (sesame butter)	¼ cup rolled oats
	2 tablespoons soy flour or soy grits
1 teaspoon vanilla	2 tablespoons dry milk powder
1 egg	½ teaspoon baking soda
	½ cup raisins

Or 1¼ cups Dynamite Mix (page 50)

Combine the butter, honey, peanut butter or tahini, vanilla, and egg in food processor, blender, or mixing bowl, and mix until smooth and creamy.

Combine the flour, wheat germ, oats, soy flour, milk powder, and baking soda and add to the wet ingredients. Blend briefly, then mix in the raisins.

Preheat oven to 325°F.

Line a cookie sheet with parchment paper or grease it with a mixture of a few drops of liquid lecithin and oil.

The cookie batter will be thick. Take pieces about the size of a walnut and press onto the cookie sheet in a diamond shape, like a kite. Bake 8 to 10 minutes or until pale gold. Remove to wire rack to cool, and store in an air-tight container so that they will retain their delicious crunchiness.

Yield: 3 dozen.

Approximately 50 calories each.

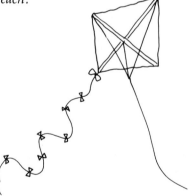

All-Star Fudgy Baseballs and Bats

These easy-to-make, unbaked, crunchy confections, full of high-mineral carob and energizing wheat germ, will help to keep you on your toes and alert when you're riding your bike, doing a dazzling pas-de-deux, taking an exam, or playing ball.

1 cup carob powder
1 cup water
¼ cup honey
¼ cup peanut butter (smooth or crunchy)
¾ cup wheat germ
¾ cup rolled oats

2 tablespoons dry milk powder
½ cup unsweetened shredded coconut
1 teaspoon cinnamon (optional)
½ teaspoon grated orange rind (optional)

In a small saucepan, combine the carob and water. Bring to a boil over low heat, stirring constantly to prevent scorching.

Add the honey and peanut butter and continue cooking for about 5 minutes, or until syrup is smooth and slightly thickened.

In a large bowl, mix together the wheat germ, oats, milk powder, coconut, cinnamon, and orange rind (if desired).

Pour about one cup of the carob syrup over the dry mixture, or as much as is needed to make a pliable, dough-like consistency. Store the remainder in the refrigerator and use as an icing or to make great milk shakes.

Pinch off pieces of the dough and roll each piece between your palms into 2-inch-long tubes about the circumference of a fountain pen, tapered at one end in the shape of a baseball bat. Roll the rest into marble-sized balls.

Yield: 18 bats and 18 balls.

Approximately 80 calories in each set.

Smart-Aleck Snaps

Full of good B vitamins that help you keep your cool, these lemon-flavored cornmeal pecan cookies perk up the lunchbox and are a delicious after-school snack. Make a big batch—they freeze well. Your kids will enjoy a few before the big game or exams.

1 cup whole wheat pastry
    flour
or ½ cup ⎰ 2 tablespoons soy flour
Dynamite ⎱ 2 tablespoons wheat germ
Mix   ⎰ 2 tablespoons bran
(page 50) ⎱ 2 tablespoons powdered milk
    ½ cup cornmeal (preferably
      Hi-lysine)
    1 teaspoon baking powder
    ½ teaspoon baking soda
    ¼ cup butter or vegetable oil
    ½ cup honey or maple syrup

1 egg
2 teaspoons finely grated
    lemon zest (lemon peel)
2 tablespoons lemon juice or
    orange juice
½ cup buttermilk, sour milk,
    or yogurt
½ cup finely chopped pecans,
    walnuts, or peanuts
chopped pecans, almonds,
    or carob chips for
    garnish (about ½ cup)

Preheat oven to 325°F.

Stir together all the dry ingredients in a bowl. In food processor, blender, or mixing bowl, beat the butter and honey together, then add the egg, lemon zest, juice, and buttermilk and process until smooth and creamy. Add the dry ingredients and mix briefly until incorporated. (If you are using an electric mixer rather than a food processor, follow the same procedure, except that you would add the buttermilk alternately with the mixture of dry ingredients.) Stir in the chopped nuts.

Drop the batter by teaspoonfuls onto an ungreased cookie sheet 2 inches apart, to allow for spreading. Garnish with nuts or carob chips. Bake for about 12 minutes. Watch the cookies carefully, as they burn easily. Remove to a wire rack to cool.

Yield: 4 dozen.

Approximately 50 calories each.

Good Scout Coconut Gems

If there are boy or girl scouts meeting at your house, they'll do their darndest to deserve these dreamy confections that will delight their tastebuds while providing the nutrients they thrive on. Use cottage cheese for more protein; cream cheese for a smoother texture—or combine the two for a velvety batter with a nutritional wallop.

BOTTOM LAYER:

¼ cup unsalted (sweet) butter, softened

¼ cup cottage cheese (drained), or cream cheese

1 teaspoon vanilla

¼ cup honey

1¼ cups whole wheat pastry flour or Dynamite Mix (page 50)

TOP LAYER:

¼ cup yogurt
3 tablespoons molasses
2 tablespoons honey
2 tablespoons dry milk powder
3 tablespoons whole wheat
   pastry flour
½ teaspoon baking soda

½ cup chopped nuts (pecans,
   walnuts, or peanuts)
½ cup sunflower seeds
1 cup unsweetened coconut
   shreds
carob chips for garnish

Preheat the oven to 325°F.

Combine the butter, cheese, vanilla, ¼ cup honey, and 1¼ cups flour in a food processor, blender, or mixing bowl. The mixture will have a dough-like consistency. Spread the batter into an 8 × 12-inch baking dish lined with parchment paper or greased with a few drops of liquid lecithin and oil. Bake for about 20 minutes.

In a medium-sized bowl, combine the yogurt, molasses, 2 tablespoons honey, milk powder, 3 tablespoons flour, baking soda, nuts, and seeds. Process or mix to combine ingredients.

Pour this mixture over the baked bottom layer (it does not have to be cooled). Top the mixture with coconut. A very nice touch would be to inscribe with carob chips the name of a boy or girl scout whose birthday is imminent. If no birthday is pending, inscribe a message such as "Scouts are tops." Bake another 10 to 15 minutes. Cut into 1½-inch squares. They'll love it!

Yield: 28 squares.

Approximately 100 calories each with the cream cheese; 85 calories each with the cottage cheese.

Muscle-Building Molasses Dreams

While nothing takes the place of exercise for building muscle power, perspiration brought on by exercise tends to deplete the body's store of minerals. These munchy yummies are divinely cakey, lavished with a velvety orange cream cheese icing (ricotta cheese can be substituted for less fat and more protein). They're also high in potassium and magnesium, because they're enriched with apricots, pumpkin, apples, and nuts. Potassium and magnesium are vital to the smooth functioning of your muscles, both mental and physical. My granddaughter says they cozy up to her tongue like mousse and ice cream.

1½ cups whole wheat pastry
flour

or ½ cup
Dynamite
Mix
(page 50)
{
¼ cup wheat germ
2 tablespoons bran
2 tablespoons milk powder
}

2 teaspoons baking soda
2 teaspoons cinnamon
½ teaspoon grated orange rind
¼ cup unsalted (sweet) butter
¼ cup honey
2 tablespoons blackstrap
molasses

2 eggs
½ cup dried apricots soaked
overnight in ½ cup
fruit juice, or ½ cup
unsweetened apricot
preserves
½ cup applesauce or chopped
apples
½ cup pumpkin puree, canned
or homemade
½ cup chopped walnuts or
sunflower seeds

CREAM CHEESE OR RICOTTA ICING

½ cup cream cheese or ricotta
cheese
½ teaspoon vanilla

2 to 3 tablespoons frozen
orange juice concentrate,
slightly thawed

Combine the flour, wheat germ, bran, milk powder, baking soda, cinnamon, and orange rind in a bowl.

In a food processor, blender, or mixing bowl, combine butter, honey, molasses, and eggs, and blend until fluffy. Add the soaked apricots or apricot preserves, applesauce or chopped apples, and pumpkin, and mix until well-combined.

Preheat oven to 350°F.

Add the flour mixture and process only until ingredients are well-combined. Fold in the nuts or seeds. Spread batter evenly in a 15 × 10-inch pan, lined with parchment paper or greased with a few drops of liquid lecithin and oil. Bake for 30 to 35 minutes, or until center springs back when lightly touched. Cool, then spread with cream cheese or ricotta icing.

To make icing: Combine cheese, vanilla, and juice concentrate in food processor, blender, or mixing bowl and mix until smooth.

Cut into diamond-shaped or rectangular bars.

Yield: 48 bars.

Approximately 55 calories each with cream cheese icing; 50 calories each with ricotta cheese.

4

SMART COOKIES
FOR THE NONSTOP
TEENAGER

At the time in their lives when they need the very best nutrition, they are getting the worst. Here's how to help them.

Even though your teenager seems to be forever eating, studies indicate that teenagers are actually the poorest-fed members of the American family. They tend to skip breakfast because they are rushed. Some will skip lunch, too, in a misguided search for a slinky figure. They tend to subsist on snacks, candy bars, and soft drinks—empty-calorie foods made chiefly of fat and sugar, woefully lacking in the vitamins, minerals, protein, and carbohydrates their growing bodies so desperately need.

What happens? Contrary to their public image, teenagers are not full of boundless vim, vigor, and exuberant good health. Many of them suffer from fatigue, anemia, scoliosis, acne, anorexia, and depression.

Help them to understand the importance of providing the right fuel for their growing bodies. Encourage good, wholesome breakfasts and sit-down meals with the family in a congenial, loving ambience, and, since they are inveterate snackers, provide them with snacks that will give their growing bodies the essential nutrients. The rewards in radiant health, upbeat attitude, and personal achievement cannot be calculated.

Battery-Charging Apricot Chews

These tasty gems, easy to stash in your purse or pocket, provide many of the nutrients often lacking in the teenage diet. Apricots and molasses provide a big dollop of iron (about 1.3 milligrams in each slice), which is especially low in the diets of teenage girls, as well as vitamin A, so important to the body's immune reaction, and calcium for growing bodies. Since these delicious confections require no baking, kids can enjoy making a quick batch for pajama party snacking.

12 dried apricots
   apple or orange juice (for soaking the apricots)
6 dried figs
½ cup raisins
½ cup almonds

½ cup sunflower seeds
2 tablespoons blackstrap molasses
½ cup wheat germ
   coconut flakes

Soak apricots and figs in apple or orange juice for a few hours or overnight. Drain. Retain juice for another purpose, or drink it.

Combine the apricots, figs, raisins, almonds, seeds, molasses, and wheat germ in food processor or blender. Process until ingredients are finely chopped.

On wax paper, form the batter into a sausage-like roll. Cover with coconut. Refrigerate for a few hours, then slice or form into balls.
Yield: 2 dozen ½-inch slices or walnut-sized balls.
Approximately 76 calories each.

Pumpkin-Seed Cookies

These cookies are chock-full of pumpkin, which is rich in vitamin A, and pumpkin seeds, which provide a bounty of zinc and calcium—nutrients essential to a lovely complexion.

1 egg
1 cup mashed pumpkin
   (canned or homemade)
¼ cup unsalted (sweet) butter
   or oil (olive or
   vegetable)
2 teaspoons vanilla
¼ cup honey
2 tablespoons molasses
1 cup whole wheat pastry
   flour

¼ cup wheat germ
2 tablespoons dry milk powder
½ teaspoon baking soda
1 teaspoon cinnamon
¼ teaspoon nutmeg
¼ teaspoon ground cloves
1½ cups rolled oats
½ cup raisins
1 cup pumpkin seeds, coarsely
   chopped

Preheat oven to 350°F.

In food processor, blender, or mixing bowl, combine the egg, pumpkin, butter or oil, vanilla, honey, and molasses. Process until smooth and creamy.

In a medium-sized bowl, combine the flour, wheat germ, milk powder, baking soda, cinnamon, nutmeg, cloves, and oats. Add to the pumpkin mixture and process briefly. Fold in the raisins and pumpkin seeds. Drop the batter by teaspoonfuls on cookie sheets lined with parchment paper or greased with a mixture of a few drops of liquid lecithin and oil. Bake for 15 minutes or until firm and golden brown. Cool on wire rack.

Yield: 4 dozen.

Approximately 45 calories each.

Pure Pleasure Maple Banana Cheesecake Tarts

A real low-calorie treat for the palate, with a bonanza of wholesome nutrients for body and soul. Soaking the sunflower seeds starts the sprouting process, which causes the nutrients to skyrocket. My ballerina granddaughter loves these, she says, "because they taste like a zillion calories but they don't make you fat!"

CRUST

½ cup sunflower seeds, soaked overnight in water

½ cup graham cracker crumbs, or your own cookie crumbs

FILLING

1 egg
1 banana
3 ounces ricotta cheese (drained) or cream cheese
1 teaspoon vanilla

1 tablespoon maple syrup granules
blueberry or strawberry preserves, unsweetened (Sorrell Ridge is a good brand)

In food processor, blender, or mixing bowl, combine sunflower seeds and crumbs. Place a teaspoon of this mixture in 12 cups of a miniature muffin pan, lined with paper liners. (You can also use regular size muffin tins.)

Preheat oven to 350°F.

Combine the egg, banana, cheese, vanilla, and maple syrup granules in mixer, blender, or food processor, and mix until smooth and creamy. Place one tablespoon of the cheese filling in each tart shell.

Bake for 20 minutes. Top each tart with a half teaspoon of fruit preserves. Store in refrigerator or freezer. Defrost a few minutes before serving.

Yield: 12 miniature tarts or 6 muffin-sized ones.

Approximately 88 calories each with cream cheese; 72 calories each with ricotta (larger tarts contain twice the calories).

Fruit and Nut Bars

Soaking the almonds starts the sprouting process, causing an explosion of nutrient values and the development of vitamin C, which helps the body utilize the calcium-rich ingredients so necessary for strong healthy bones. The pineapple, dates, and coconut provide a medley of flavors to delight your taste buds.

2 eggs
*½ cup drained crushed
    pineapple (reserve juice)*
*½ cup almonds soaked in
    reserved pineapple juice
    (for 2 hours or overnight)*
*¼ cup molasses or
    honey*

½ cup chopped dates
*½ cup shredded coconut,
    unsweetened*
*½ cup whole wheat pastry
    flour*
¼ cup dry milk powder
¼ cup wheat germ

Drain the crushed pineapple, reserving the juice, and soak the almonds in the juice for two hours or overnight.

Preheat oven to 350°F.

In food processor, blender, or mixing bowl, combine eggs, pineapple, almonds, molasses, dates, and coconut, and mix until well-combined. Add the flour, milk powder, and wheat germ, and mix briefly.

Spread the mixture in a 9-inch-square baking dish lined with parchment paper or greased with a few drops of liquid lecithin and oil. Bake for 30 minutes or until golden and firm. Cool slightly, then cut into 1½-inch squares.

Yield: 36 squares.

Approximately 45 calories each.

Energy-Packed Date and Sesame Brownies

Chewy date-and-nut filling between the crunchy layers of these brownies make them an ambrosial treat, bound to boost your morale and your energy quotient.

2 eggs	1 teaspoon baking powder
¼ cup honey	¾ cup sesame seeds
¼ cup butter	1 cup pitted dates, finely
¼ cup milk	chopped
¼ cup carob powder	½ cup raisins
¼ cup whole wheat flour	½ cup chopped nuts or
¼ cup wheat germ	sunflower seeds
2 tablespoons dry milk powder	

Preheat oven to 325°F.

In food processor, blender, or mixing bowl, combine eggs, honey, butter, and milk. Blend until smooth and creamy.

In a mixing bowl, combine carob powder, flour, wheat germ, milk powder, baking powder and sesame seeds. Add to the egg mixture and process just until ingredients are well-blended.

In another bowl, combine the dates, raisins, and nuts. Pour half the batter into a baking pan about 8 × 13 inches, lined with parchment paper or greased with a mixture of liquid lecithin and oil.

Spread the mixture of dates, raisins, and nuts over the bottom layer, then cover with the rest of the batter. Bake for 30 minutes. Allow to cool slightly, then cut into 2-inch squares.

Yield: 32 squares.

Approximately 90 calories each.

5

SMART COOKIES
THAT GO TO COLLEGE
Survival Snacks

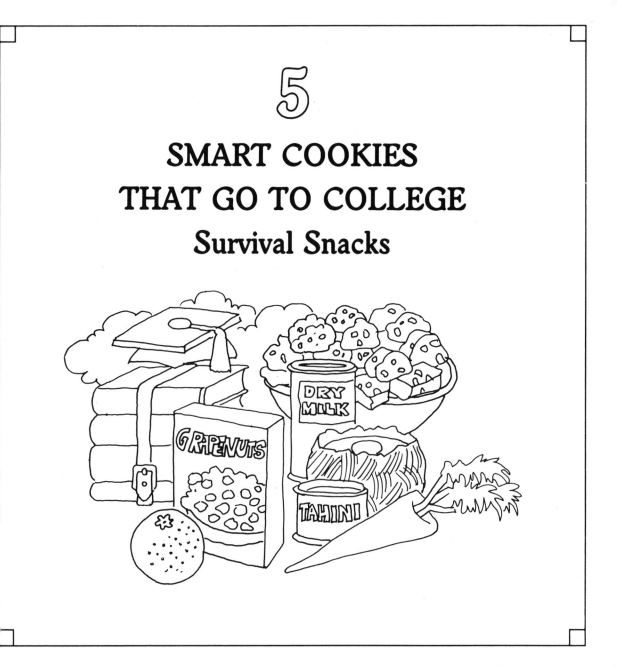

The food in most college dining rooms is usually highly salted, highly sugared, over-processed, and lacking in the nutrients essential to health and vitality. I receive letters about it from students all over the country. "The food here is awful," they say. "I find myself filling up on starches, my skin is breaking out, I'm always tired, and I have trouble keeping up with my work."

The college years can be a real drain on the body's resources, and when the body lacks even one essential nutrient, the mind may suffer a slow-down.

When our kids were at college, I used to send what they call "Mom's Care Packages"—dried fruit, homemade granola, vitamin C tablets, and cookies, cookies, cookies.

As a footnote, I must mention that our kids missed very few days due to illness; all four made the dean's list and three of them qualified for Phi Beta Kappa.

To mail cookies, stack them tightly in a tin box with a tight-fitting lid or in a sturdy cardboard box. Use plenty of filler material in the bottom of the container, on top of the cookies, and in all the empty spaces. Filler can be crushed waxed paper or foil, but the filler our kids liked best was popcorn. It's lightweight, it provides good insulation against breakage, and it's edible.

On-The-Go Fruit and Granola Bars

High-fiber oats contribute to the powerhouse of energizing nutrients in these toothsome temptations.

2 cups rolled oats
½ cup coarsely chopped nuts
    (walnuts, pecans,
    filberts, peanuts, or
    sunflower seeds)
½ cup raisins
1 teaspoon cinnamon

2 tablespoons butter
¼ cup honey, molasses, or
    barley malt syrup (or a
    combination of all three)
2 tablespoons apple juice
1 banana, mashed
1 egg, beaten

Preheat oven to 350°F.

In a medium-sized bowl, combine oats, nuts, raisins, and cinnamon. Set aside.

In a saucepan, melt the butter and honey. Add the juice and pour this mixture over the dry ingredients. Blend in the mashed banana, then the egg. Press the batter into a 9-inch-square baking dish lined with parchment paper or greased with a mixture of a few drops of liquid lecithin and oil. Bake for 20 to 25 minutes. Cool slightly, then cut into 1½-inch squares.

Yield: 25 squares.

Approximately 75 calories each.

Maple Walnut Nuggets

The lovely flavor of maple and the delicious crunch of walnuts make these little gems a welcome and wholesome companion for-late night cramming.

3 tablespoons butter	2 tablespoons milk
1 egg	½ teaspoon baking powder
¼ cup maple syrup granules	¼ teaspoon nutmeg
½ teaspoon vanilla	¼ cup currants
¾ cup rolled oats	¼ cup chopped nuts
½ cup whole wheat pastry flour	

Combine oats and milk and let the mixture stand.

In food processor, blender, or mixing bowl, cream together the butter, maple granules, egg, and vanilla. Combine flour, baking powder, and nutmeg, and blend with the creamed mixture. Stir in the oat mixture, the currants, and the nuts.

Preheat oven to 375°F.

Drop the batter by teaspoonfuls on a cookie sheet lined with parchment paper or greased with a mixture of a few drops liquid lecithin and oil. Bake for about 10 minutes or until lightly browned. Let stand a minute, then remove to wire rack to cool.

Yield: 2 dozen.

Approximately 55 calories each.

Fig and Sesame Snacks

These no-bake, crunchy bars, made from cereal, milk, fruit, and other goodies, will substitute for breakfast or reinforce a skimpy one when you're rushed—but the taste may have you nibbling 'round the clock.

½ cup honey
½ cup peanut butter
2 tablespoons unsalted (sweet) butter
½ cup chopped figs (raisins may be substituted)

½ cup dry milk powder
2½ cups Grapenuts cereal
1 tablespoon grated orange rind
3 tablespoons sesame seeds, toasted

In a saucepan, over low heat, blend the honey, peanut butter, and butter. Remove from heat and stir in the chopped figs or raisins. Add the dry milk and Grapenuts, and mix well. Press firmly into a 9-inch-square pan. Sprinkle with sesame seeds and press them in. Cool for one hour, then cut into 1½-inch squares. Keep refrigerated or frozen.
Yield: 25 squares.
Approximately 130 calories each.

Munchable Orange Wheat Germ Gems

These little gems have what it takes to keep your body and mind functioning in high gear—fiber, protein, vitamins, minerals, and the bioflavinoids, provided by the orange rind, which go to bat for your immune system. The cookies freeze well, travel well, and taste swell.

½ cup oil (preferably olive)
½ cup honey
2 eggs
1 cup steamed carrots, chopped
1 teaspoon vanilla
⅓ cup wheat germ
¾ cup whole wheat pastry
    flour

¼ cup soy flour
½ cup coconut shreds
2 tablespoons cornmeal
    (preferably Hi-lysine)
2 tablespoons oat bran or
    rolled oats
2 tablespoons grated orange
    rind

In food processor, blender, or mixing bowl, cream together oil, honey, eggs, and vanilla. Add carrots and blend. In another bowl, combine the flours, wheat germ, cornmeal, coconut, orange rind, and oats. Add to creamed mixture and blend.

Preheat oven to 350°F.

Drop batter by teaspoonfuls on a cookie sheet lined with parchment paper or greased with a few drops of liquid lecithin and oil. Bake for 18 to 20 minutes.

Yield: 3 dozen.

Approximately 65 calories each.

Tahini Oatmeal Walnut Cookies

Tahini, made from sesame seeds and available in specialty food shops and many supermarkets, is an excellent source of essential fatty acids, so important to smooth beautiful skin, healthy hair, and to preventing damaging deposits of cholesterol. These cookies have long been a favorite in our cookie jar; they also freeze and travel like troupers.

6 tablespoons tahini
½ cup honey
½ teaspoon cinnamon

½ cup chopped walnuts
1 cup rolled oats

Preheat oven to 325°F.

In a medium-sized mixing bowl, stir tahini and honey together. Add the nuts, then the oatmeal sprinkled with the cinnamon, and mix to blend ingredients.

Drop the batter by teaspoonfuls on a cookie sheet lined with parchment paper or greased with a few drops of liquid lecithin and oil. Bake for 10 to 12 minutes.

Yield: 2½ to 3 dozen.

Approximately 40 calories each.

6

IN PRAISE OF VEGETABLES

Many years ago a cartoon in the *New Yorker* depicted a small, grumpy little girl glowering at her dinner plate. "I say it's spinach," she said, "and I say the hell with it."

That pretty much sums up most children's and many adults' attitude toward vegetables.

You can tell veggie-avoiders from now till tomorrow that vegetables, both raw and cooked, are storehouses of vitamins and minerals, that they are high-fiber, low-calorie, low-fat, and rich in complex carbohydrates, that they contain substances that seem to deter the development of cancer, that they are knights in shiny multicolored armor that can protect us from some life-threatening conditions. And what do you get? A hoarse voice and a pile of leftovers.

Relax! With these delicious cookies, you'll never again have to lecture, nag or beg. They'll eat their vegetables and love every bite.

Golden Carrot Molasses Gems

Carrots, with their rich payload of carotene—now recognized as an important anti-cancer agent—team up with oats, bran, and wheat germ to make these cookies the perfect high-fiber munch.

⅓ cup vegetable oil (preferably olive)
⅓ cup molasses
1 egg
1 teaspoon vanilla
1 cup grated raw carrots
½ cup whole wheat pastry flour
¼ cup wheat germ
2 tablespoons bran
2 tablespoons rice polish or soy flour
½ teaspoon baking powder
1 teaspoon baking soda
½ teaspoon nutmeg
1 teaspoon cinnamon
¼ cup dry milk powder
⅔ cup raisins
1¼ cups rolled oats

In food processor, blender, or mixing bowl, combine oil, molasses, egg, and vanilla. Blend until smooth and creamy. Add carrots, and blend.

Combine the wheat flour, wheat germ, bran, rice polish or soy flour, baking powder, baking soda, nutmeg, cinnamon, and milk powder. Add to the carrot mixture. Blend briefly until incorporated. Stir in the raisins and the oats.

Preheat oven to 350°F.

Drop the batter by tablespoonfuls onto a cookie sheet lined with parchment paper or greased with a mixture of liquid lecithin and oil. Bake for 12 to 15 minutes.

Yield: 3 dozen.

Approximately 60 calories each.

Zucchini-Spice Squares

Zucchini lovers—and veggie avoiders—never had it so good. Sprouting the garbanzo beans causes an explosion of nutrients and the development of vitamin B12, which is very rare in vegetables. The flour, made by grinding the dried sprouts in a seed mill or coffee grinder, makes these low-calorie confections a high-energy food. The combination of grains and beans greatly enhances the biological value of the protein.

1 egg	2 tablespoons soy flour or
4 tablespoons unsalted (sweet)	flour made from dried
butter	garbanzo sprouts
¼ cup honey	(instructions follow)
1½ teaspoons vanilla	1 teaspoon baking powder
1 cup grated zucchini	1½ teaspoons cinnamon
1 cup whole wheat pastry	¼ teaspoon ginger
flour, minus 2 tablespoons	¼ teaspoon nutmeg
2 tablespoons wheat germ	½ cup chopped nuts

Preheat oven to 350°F.

In food processor, blender, or mixing bowl, blend egg, butter, honey, and vanilla until smooth and creamy. Add the zucchini and mix to combine. In a bowl, combine flour, wheat germ, soy or garbanzo bean flour, baking powder, cinnamon, ginger, and nutmeg. Mix to blend ingredients. Stir in the nuts.

Spread the batter in a 9-inch-square baking dish, lined with parchment paper or greased with a few drops of liquid lecithin and oil.

Bake for 30 minutes. Cut into 1½-inch squares.
Yield: 25 squares.
Approximately 65 calories each.

SPROUTED GARBANZO BEAN FLOUR

Soak ½ cup garbanzo beans in about 2 cups of water overnight. Next morning, pour off the water. (Save it and use it in soup—it contains valuable vitamins and minerals.) Rinse the beans and spread them out in a colander. Dampen a dish towel or two layers of paper towels, and place over the beans. Slip the whole thing into a plastic bag to retain moisture, but leave it open at one end to ensure a source of oxygen.

Remove the covering and rinse the beans several times a day. In two or three days, you will have sprouted garbanzos.

To make the flour, spread the sprouted garbanzos out on a baking sheet and then dry them in a gas oven by the heat of the pilot light or in an electric oven heated to 250°F, then turned off. Don't put the beans in the oven until you turn it off. Leave them for about 6 hours. If they are not thoroughly dried, remove them from the oven and raise the temperature again to 250°F, turn off the oven, and repeat.

When the sprouted beans are thoroughly dried, grind them in a seed mill, blender, or food processor.

Halloween Pumpkin-Raisin Goodies

Your kids might choose to stay home for these instead of hazarding the Trick or Treat route. Try serving these at your own Halloween party—the results will surprise you!

4 tablespoons butter
¼ cup honey
1 egg
1 teaspoon vanilla
1 cup canned or pureed
    cooked pumpkin
1 cup whole wheat pastry
    flour
½ cup wheat germ

½ cup rolled oats
1 teaspoon baking soda
1 teaspoon cinnamon
½ teaspoon ginger
½ teaspoon nutmeg
¾ cup raisins
½ cup pecans or walnuts,
    chopped

Preheat oven to 350°F.

In food processor, blender, or mixing bowl, blend together the butter, honey, egg, and vanilla. Add pumpkin and blend to incorporate. In a bowl, combine flour, wheat germ, rolled oats, baking soda, cinnamon, ginger, and nutmeg. Mix briefly to blend ingredients. Stir in raisins and nuts.

For large cookies, drop the batter by tablespoonfuls onto a cookie sheet lined with parchment paper or greased with liquid lecithin and oil. For small cookies, drop by the teaspoonful. Bake for 15 to 20 minutes.
Yield: 2 dozen large cookies or 4 dozen small cookies.
Approximately 90 calories in the large, 45 in the small.

Parsnip Pecan Cookies

Parsnips are a good source of iron and potassium and have a natural sweetness that precludes the use of very much concentrated sweetener, greatly reducing the calorie content of these delicious confections.

1 egg
2 tablespoons honey
⅓ cup oil
1 teaspoon vanilla
1 cup cooked parsnips, sieved
1 cup whole wheat pastry
    flour, minus two
    tablespoons

2 tablespoons soy flour
½ cup wheat germ
2 teaspoons baking powder
½ cup chopped pecans
½ cup raisins
2 tablespoons sesame seeds

In food processor, blender, or mixing bowl, combine oil, honey, egg, parsnips, and vanilla. Mix until smooth and creamy. In another bowl, combine the flours, wheat germ, and baking powder, and add to the wet ingredients. Blend. Stir in the nuts, raisins, and seeds.

Preheat oven to 350°F.

Drop the batter by tablespoonfuls on a cookie sheet lined with parchment paper or greased with liquid lecithin and oil. Bake for 12 to 15 minutes or until lightly browned.

Yield: 3 dozen.

Approximately 60 calories each.

7
SMART COOKIES
ON THE RUN

Everyone's on an exercise kick. Walking, jogging, swimming, aerobics, weight training, and running, running, running!

Great—for the cardiovascular system, for grace of body, for an upbeat attitude, for clarity of mind, for improving one's self-image. But beware of the mineral blues. If you feel weak and tired, it may be that you're sweating away some important minerals, especially potassium, magnesium, and zinc. You may also be losing some important vitamins—riboflavin (B2), which is necessary to convert food into energy, thiamine (B1), sometimes called the morale vitamin because it helps you achieve an upbeat attitude, and pyridoxine (B6), which helps prevent anemia and may play a role in increasing muscle endurance.

The cookies I've dished up for very active people are rich in all the B vitamins, and in potassium, so necessary for healthy nerves and muscles; in magnesium, needed for strong bones and teeth; and in zinc, which aids in the healing of wounds, helps prevent prostate problems, and promotes normal growth and development in children.

Whew! With all this going for you, you might not expect the final payoff—the wonderful textures and delightful taste combinations of these Smart Cookies. Enjoy them even when you're taking the day off!

Almond Delights

Just a hint of peppermint gives these confections a surprisingly refreshing flavor. The almonds, soaked to multiply their vitamin values, provide a delectable crunch and lots of magnesium.

1 egg
1/3 cup honey
1/2 teaspoon vanilla
1/4 teaspoon peppermint extract
1/2 cup whole wheat pastry
    flour, minus 2 tablespoons

2 tablespoons wheat germ
1/4 teaspoon baking soda
1/2 cup pre-soaked almonds,
    drained and chopped

Soak the almonds overnight in water to cover.

Preheat oven to 325°F.

In food processor, blender, or mixing bowl, blend together the egg, honey, vanilla, and peppermint extract.

In a small bowl, combine flour, wheat germ, and baking soda. Add to the egg mixture and blend briefly. Stir in chopped nuts. Pour batter into an 8-inch-square baking dish, lined with parchment paper or greased with a mixture of a few drops of liquid lecithin and oil. Bake for 25 to 30 minutes. Cool slightly, then cut into 2-inch squares.
Yields: 16 squares.

Approximately 65 calories each.

Long-Distance Sunflower Banana Fig Sandwiches

A dynamic trio—sunflower seeds have what it takes to turn you on and get you going (lots of B vitamins, zinc, and magnesium); bananas are an excellent source of potassium and vitamin B6; and figs contain not only iron, magnesium, and potassium, but are an excellent source of bone-building calcium, even more than milk. The yeast, wheat germ, molasses, and peanut butter further enhance the nutrient value of these delicious, crunchy confections.

SANDWICH WAFERS

½ cup peanut butter
2 tablespoons molasses
2 tablespoons honey
1 banana
1 egg
1 teaspoon vanilla
1¼ cups whole wheat pastry flour
2 tablespoons brewer's yeast
2 tablespoons wheat germ
¾ teaspoon baking soda
½ cup sunflower seeds, ground
½ cup whole sunflower seeds, for topping

ORANGE-FIG SPREAD

1 cup dried figs
¼ cup water
6 tablespoons frozen orange juice concentrate

Combine peanut butter, molasses, honey, egg, banana, and vanilla in food processor, blender, or mixing bowl, and blend until smooth and creamy. In another bowl, combine flour, yeast, wheat germ, and baking soda and blend with the first mixture until well-combined. Chill the dough, tightly covered, for an hour.

Preheat oven to 350°F.

Pinch off pieces of dough about the size of a walnut, dip them in the ground sunflower seeds, then flatten the chunks between your hands to make circles about 2 inches in diameter. Place on a cookie sheet lined with parchment paper or greased with a few drops of liquid lecithin and oil. Top each wafer with a few whole sunflower seeds. Bake for 7 to 9 minutes or until firm.

To make the orange-fig spread, cook the figs in water until tender (about 8 minutes). Combine the cooked figs with the orange juice concentrate in blender or food processor, and process until of spreadable consistency.

Spread the flat side of half the cooled wafers with orange-fig spread. Top with the remaining wafers.

Yield: 12 sandwiches.

Approximately 236 calories each.

Poppy Seed Carob Confections

Those tiny black poppy seeds are little dynamos of vitality; and a good source of the B vitamins and many minerals, including zinc. The currants provide iron and the carob is an excellent source of potassium.

1 cup poppy seeds
½ cup hot milk
¼ cup butter
¼ cup honey
¼ cup carob syrup (recipe
    follows)
1 cup whole wheat pastry
    flour

2 tablespoons wheat germ
2 tablespoons bran
½ teaspoon cinnamon
¼ teaspoon cloves
1 cup currants

Place poppy seeds in a small bowl and add the hot milk. Set aside. In food processor, blender, or mixing bowl, cream butter and honey. Add the carob syrup and the poppy seed mixture. Blend well.

In a small bowl combine flour, wheat germ, bran, cinnamon, and cloves, and mix well. Stir in the currants.

Preheat oven to 350°F.

Drop the batter by teaspoonfuls on to a cookie sheet lined with parchment paper or greased with a mixture of liquid lecithin and oil. Bake for 15 to 20 minutes.

Yield: 3 dozen.

Approximately 65 calories each.

CAROB SYRUP

Combine ½ cup carob powder and ½ cup water in a small saucepan. Bring to a boil over low heat, stirring constantly. Add 2 tablespoons honey and 1 tablespoon butter and cook for about 6 minutes, or until smooth and slightly thickened. Cool. May be made ahead and stored in refrigerator.

8
SMART COOKIES
FOR EXECUTIVES

Your personal stock has its ups and downs—and, obviously, no cookie is going to elevate the downs. The right cookie *can* affect the way you feel about the downs, however.

These "boardroom cookies" are rich in the nutrients that help you handle the stress that comes with success. Munch a few in both the good times and the trying moments, and you'll feel like my stockbroker, who said between bites, "The only thing that gets me down is the elevator."

Dow Jones Banana Chips

These high-fiber, low-fat gems have what it takes to boost your stock, improve your performance, and maximize your potential. Enjoy them with Perrier, milk, or a nice hot beverage.

1 egg
¼ cup unsalted (sweet) butter
¼ cup honey
1 banana
2 teaspoons vanilla
1 tablespoon water
1 cup whole wheat pastry
 flour
¼ cup bran
¼ cup rice polish or soy
 flour
3 tablespoons wheat germ
1 teaspoon baking powder
½ cup granola (page 29)
½ cup chopped nuts or raisins
½ cup carob chips

Preheat oven to 350°F.

In food processor, blender, or mixing bowl, blend together until smooth the egg, butter, honey, banana, vanilla, and water. In another bowl, combine the flour, bran, rice polish or soy flour, wheat germ, and baking powder. Add to the first mixture and blend briefly, just enough to combine ingredients. Stir in granola, nuts or raisins, and carob chips. Drop the batter by tablespoonfuls on a cookie sheet lined with parchment paper or greased with a mixture of a few drops of liquid lecithin and oil. Bake for 12 to 15 minutes.

Yield: 3 dozen.

Approximately 55 calories each.

Second-Wind Sesame Chews

A pick-me-up cookie that won't let you down, these easy-to-make unbaked bonbons, flavored with tahini, contribute a healthy dividend of linoleic acid, so important to the utilization of fats, a nice complexion, and a healthy prostate gland. Sprouting the wheat berries causes an explosion of the B vitamins, which boost morale and jack up energy.

3 tablespoons tahini
3 tablespoons honey or
* molasses*
½ cup wheat sprouts
* (see page 37)*

½ cup chopped pecans
½ cup shredded coconut
3 tablespoons carob powder
3 tablespoons sunflower seeds,
* crushed*

Combine tahini and honey. Add sprouts, pecans, and coconut and form into 1-inch balls. Roll each ball first in carob powder, then in sunflower meal. Store in freezer.
Yield: 18 chews.
Approximately 55 calories each.

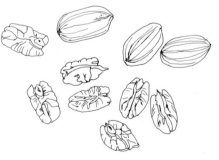

Double-Good Nougat Bars

You'll feel like everything's going your way when you bite into one of these gooey, chewy bars that cozy up to your tongue with all the wonderful nostalgia of an old-fashioned nut caramel.

4 tablespoons peanut butter
(smooth or chunky)
4 tablespoons honey
½ cup raisins
½ cup sunflower seeds or
chopped nuts (or a
mixture of both)

⅓ cup shredded coconut
½ cup carob syrup (page 95)
3 cups Rice Krispies, corn
puff cereal, or any dry
cereal (chow mein noodles
can also be used)

Combine peanut butter and honey. Add raisins, seeds or nuts, coconut, and dry cereal. Spread mixture in a 9-inch-square pan lined with parchment paper or greased with a mixture of liquid lecithin and oil. Spread wax paper over the batter and pat it down evenly. Remove the wax paper and pour the carob syrup over the top. Chill about one hour, then cut into 2-inch bars.

Yield: 3 dozen.

Approximately 45 calories each.

T.G.I.F. Almond-Kahlua Squares

The spirit of a holiday weekend is captured in these exotically flavored, crunchy confections topped with toasted almonds and filled, if you like, with orange-fig spread.

2 eggs
⅓ cup unsalted (sweet) butter
⅓ cup honey
⅓ cup carob syrup (page 95)
1 teaspoon vanilla
2 tablespoons Kahlua or rum
1¼ cup whole wheat pastry flour

¼ cup wheat germ
2 teaspoons baking powder
¾ cup coarsely chopped toasted almonds
apricot preserves or orange-fig spread (optional)

Preheat oven to 325°F.

In food processor, blender, or mixing bowl, blend together the eggs, butter, honey, carob syrup, vanilla, and Kahlua until smooth. Combine the flour, wheat germ, and baking powder, and add to the egg mixture. Stir in ½ cup almonds.

Spread mixture in a 13 × 9-inch baking pan lined with parchment paper or greased with a mixture of liquid lecithin and oil. Sprinkle remaining almonds on top. Bake for 25 to 30 minutes. Cool in pan, then cut into 1½-inch squares while still warm.

Yield: 35 squares.

Approximately 60 calories each.

Alternate presentation: Slice squares in half horizontally. Spread one half of the squares on the cut side with apricot preserves, spiked with

a little Kahlua, and press together like a sandwich. Instead of apricot preserves, you could use orange-fig spread (see page 92).
Approximately 65 calories each.

Sesame-Raisin Serenity Squares

You'll be bullish for these crunchy cookies, chock-full of pantothenic acid and all the B vitamins that help you keep your cool.

⅓ cup tahini	¼ cup rice polish
½ cup honey, molasses, or barley malt syrup	¼ cup wheat germ
	½ cup shredded coconut
2 eggs	¼ cup sesame seeds
1 cup rolled oats	1 cup raisins

Preheat oven to 350°F.

In food processor, blender, or mixing bowl, blend together tahini, honey, and eggs until smooth and creamy. Add the oats, rice polish, wheat germ, coconut, and seeds, and process or mix until ingredients are well-combined. Stir in the raisins.

Spread the batter in a 9-inch-square baking dish lined with parchment paper or greased with liquid lecithin and oil. Bake for 20 minutes or until toasty brown. Cut in 1½-inch squares and remove to the cooling rack.

Yield: 25 squares.
Approximately 85 calories each.

9

BLESS-YOUR-HEART COOKIES

While all the cookies in this book are kind to your heart—they don't burden you with the negatives shown to be a drag on the cardiovascular system (salt, sugar, and hydrogenated fats)—the cookies in this chapter are a special blessing. They are jazzed up with nutrients that lower the levels of "bad" cholesterol—low-density lipoprotein (LDL) —which is associated with increased risk of heart attacks. And they increase levels of high-density proteins (HDL), thought to protect against heart attacks.

In the same delicious morsel, you will be getting an added bonus of helpful fiber and vitamin E, which has been shown to help maintain normal viscosity in the blood, thus lessening the risk of blood clots which could cause heart attacks and strokes.

And that's not all. They also contain the anti-coronary ingredients of the famous breakfast mash developed by research chemist Jacobus Rinse, Ph.D.

Having suffered a debilitating angina attack at the age of 51 and been given a medical prognosis of 10 years of restricted activity, Dr. Rinse put his genius to work and developed his now-famous heart-saving formula—lecithin granules, brewer's yeast, wheat germ, and sunflower seeds. Dr. Rinse is now in his eighties and recently took up skiing.

Crunchy and nutty, and with a hint of oranges and carob, these cookies are also nutritious goldmines. Enjoy them to your heart's content.

Hale and Hearty Confections
À La Dr. Rinse's Formula

With these delectable confections, you will not only give your heart a break, you will delight your palate. Eight a day will give you all the ingredients of Dr. Rinse's formula in the correct proportions, in a deliciously enjoyable way.

3 tablespoons frozen orange juice concentrate, slightly thawed
2 tablespoons honey
3 heaping tablespoons peanut butter (smooth or chunky)
3 tablespoons wheat germ

3 tablespoons lecithin granules
3 tablespoons brewer's yeast
3 tablespoons carob powder
3 tablespoons sunflower seeds
3 teaspoons dry milk powder
2 tablespoons bran
2 tablespoons sesame seeds

In a food processor, blender, or mixing bowl, blend together the orange juice, honey, and peanut butter. Mix in the wheat germ, lecithin, yeast, carob, sunflower seeds, dry milk powder, bran, and sesame seeds. Form into a dough. If it doesn't hold together, add a little hot water. Break off pieces the size of small walnuts and form into the shape of kisses. Serve with love.
Yield: 24.
Approximately 45 calories each.

Heart-to-Heart Chewy Nuggets

These nutty, chewy treats will delight your palate and gladden your heart. They are enriched with olive oil, a mono-unsaturate, which was recently shown to be a winner in the cholesterol wars—even better than the polyunsaturates, which tend to lower both the bad and the good cholesterol levels. The mono-unsaturates, on the other hand, lower the LDL, which is associated with increased risk of heart attack, but don't touch the HDL, which *The Journal of Lipid Research* reports is thought to protect against heart attacks.

¼ *cup olive oil*	2 *tablespoons wheat germ*
¼ *cup honey*	½ *teaspoon cinnamon*
1 *egg*	1 *tablespoon grated orange*
1 *teaspoon vanilla*	*rind*
⅓ *cup whole wheat pastry*	¼ *cup sunflower seeds*
flour	½ *cup rolled oats*
2 *tablespoons lecithin granules*	½ *cup chopped nuts*

Preheat oven to 350°F.

In food processor, blender, or mixing bowl, combine oil, honey, egg, and vanilla. Process or mix until smooth and creamy. Add flour, lecithin, wheat germ, cinnamon, orange rind, sunflower seeds, and rolled oats. Blend until combined.

Spoon batter into a 9-inch-square baking pan lined with parchment paper or greased with a mixture of liquid lecithin and oil. Sprinkle nuts over the batter. Bake for 20 to 25 minutes, or until toothpick

inserted in center comes out clean. Cool slightly, then cut into 1½-inch squares.
Yield: 25 squares.
Approximately 70 calories each.

Fruit and Nut Gems

A special treat for those who cannot tolerate concentrated sweeteners, these naturally sweet munchies deliver a big jolt of potassium, a mineral vital to the rhythmic beat of your heart.

1 cup raisins	*3 tablespoons wheat germ*
1 cup chopped prunes	*2 tablespoons lecithin granules*
1½ cups chopped walnuts	*3 eggs, lightly beaten*

Preheat oven to 350°F.

In a mixing bowl, combine raisins, prunes, nuts, wheat germ, and lecithin granules. Add the beaten eggs and mix well.

Spoon the batter into the cups of two muffin tins lined with paper liners or greased with a mixture of liquid lecithin and oil. Bake for 20 to 25 minutes.
Yield: 2 dozen miniature fruitcakes.
Approximately 95 calories each.

Heart's Delight Tahini Strawberry Roll-Ups

You can nibble these to your heart's content. Tahini (sesame butter) has no cholesterol but lots of unsaturated fatty acids, which help metabolize cholesterol. It is also an exceptionally good source of methionine, which complements the amino acids of the other ingredients, making these confections a source of protein of high biological value.

¼ cup tahini
¼ cup unsweetened strawberry
   preserves (Sorrell Ridge
   is a good brand)
2 tablespoons lecithin granules
2 tablespoons wheat germ
2 tablespoons unsweetened
   shredded coconut

¼ cup sunflower seeds
1 tablespoon carob powder
   (optional)
2 tablespoons sesame seeds,
   lightly toasted

In a small bowl mix together tahini and preserves. Mix in the lecithin, wheat germ, coconut, and sunflower seeds. The batter should be fairly stiff.

Pinch off pieces the size of a hazelnut and roll into balls. Roll the balls first in sesame seeds and then in carob, if you choose. Or, for variety, roll some only in carob and some only in seeds.

Yield: 2 dozen.

Approximately 35 calories each.

High-Fiber Buckwheat Buckaroos

These cookies have it all: olive oil to tame cholesterol levels; fiber to prevent constipation and stress; wheat germ for vitamin E; applesauce for pectin, which slows down the digestion of cholesterol-rich foods and helps to detoxify the body; and lecithin granules, your heart's best friend. Live it up—your ticker (and taste buds) never had it so good!

1 egg
¼ cup olive oil
¼ cup honey
1 cup unsweetened applesauce
1 cup whole wheat pastry
    flour
1 teaspoon baking soda
¼ cup wheat germ
½ teaspoon baking powder
¼ cup bran
3 tablespoons lecithin granules

1 teaspoon cinnamon
¼ teaspoon ground cloves
¼ teaspoon freshly grated
    nutmeg
¼ cup raisins
½ cup uncooked buckwheat
    groats (also known as
    kasha, and available at
    supermarkets and health-
    food stores)
½ cup rolled oats

In food processor, blender, or mixing bowl, blend together the egg, olive oil, and honey until smooth and creamy. Add the applesauce and blend it into the batter. In another bowl, combine the flour, baking soda, wheat germ, baking powder, bran, lecithin, cinnamon, cloves, and nutmeg. Add to the batter and blend briefly, just to integrate ingredients. Stir in the raisins, groats, and oats.

Preheat oven to 350°F.

Drop the batter by teaspoonfuls on cookie sheets lined with parchment paper or greased with a mixture of liquid lecithin and oil. Bake for 10 to 12 minutes.

Yield: 4 dozen.

Approximately 40 calories each.

10

RECIPES FOR A
ROMANTIC EVENING

Want to keep the magic in your marriage? Set the stage for an enchanted evening with candlelight and wine and soft romantic music, but do your homework in the kitchen. Make up a batch of cookies rich in such delicious turn-ons as almonds, strawberries, raisins, and coconuts. Like all Smart Cookies, the following treats are loaded with vitamins and minerals, such as thiamine, niacin, potassium, and zinc, which help orchestrate a woman's metabolism and ward off impotence in men.

I confess—the cookies in this chapter are wickedly seductive. Try them during tea for two, on a getaway picnic in the country, or for a midnight snack. They might help make your honeymoon last forever!

Live-It-Up Carob Walnut Halvah

Women in ancient Babylonia ate halvah to enhance their sex appeal, and now research gives scientific support to this old folklore. Potassium in the sesame seeds and aspartic acid in the honey provide nutrients that help relieve chronic fatigue and stimulate interest in love-making!

¼ cup tahini
¼ cup honey
½ cup unsweetened shredded
   coconut
½ cup wheat germ

½ cup sunflower seeds
½ teaspoon cinnamon
 2 tablespoons carob powder
¼ cup crushed walnuts
   (optional)

In a medium-sized bowl, blend together the tahini and honey. Using a seed mill or blender, grind the coconut, wheat germ, and sunflower seeds very fine. Combine with the tahini mixture. Add the carob and cinnamon and knead the mixture into a ball of dough.

Separate the dough into 4 parts. Roll each part into a roll about 1 inch in diameter, and coat with walnuts if you choose to use them. Wrap each roll separately in wax paper and refrigerate. Cut into ½-inch slices as needed.

Yield: 4 rolls, each 6 inches in length. Each roll yields 12 slices.
Approximately 50 calories per ½-inch slice.

Spice-of-Life Pumpkin-Seed Squares

The zinc in these pumpkiny confections can really help put some pow in your love life.

¼ cup tahini (sesame butter)	1½ cups Grapenuts cereal
¼ cup honey	⅓ cup pumpkin seeds
1 tablespoon butter	3 dried apricots, snipped into small
2 tablespoons dry milk	pieces
½ cup raisins	1 tablespoon shredded coconut

In a saucepan over low heat, blend tahini, honey, and butter. Add raisins. Remove from heat. Add dry milk and Grapenuts. Press the mixture firmly into a 9-inch-square pan. Press pumpkin seeds and snipped apricots over the surface. Garnish with the coconut. Cool for about an hour, then cut into 1½-inch squares. Keep refrigerated. Bring to room temperature before serving.

Yield: 25 squares.

Approximately 75 calories each.

Love-In-Bloom Fruit and Nut Squares

These tasty tidbits give you a big jolt of potassium, calcium, and magnesium.

2 cups dried fruits (raisins, dates, prunes, and figs)
½ cup nuts (cashews, pecans, almonds, or walnuts)
2 tablespoons carob powder
1 tablespoon honey
wheat germ, coconut, or sesame seeds (about ¾ cup)
whole almonds, cashews, or walnuts for garnish

Chop fruit and ½ cup nuts in food mill, blender, or food processor. Mix in carob and honey.

Pinch off walnut-sized pieces, roll them in wheat germ, coconut, or sesame seeds, and press into a square. Top each piece with an almond, a half cashew, or a piece of walnut.

Yield: 2 dozen.

Approximately 55 calories each.

Almond Crescents

A delicious prop for a romantic evening, these melt-in-your-mouth cookies are loaded with crunchy almonds, a good source of vitamin E and potassium.

¼ cup vegetable oil (preferably olive)
¼ cup butter
¼ cup honey
1 teaspoon vanilla
½ cup whole wheat pastry flour

½ cup sunflower seed flour
¼ cup wheat germ
1 cup almonds, ground to a flour
½ cup almonds, chopped

In food processor, blender, or mixing bowl, blend oil, butter, honey, and vanilla till smooth and creamy. Combine the whole wheat flour, sunflower seed flour, wheat germ, and almond flour, and add to the mixture. Blend. Chill dough for about a half hour.

Preheat oven to 325°F.

Pinch off walnut-sized chunks of dough and shape into crescents. Dip each crescent in chopped almonds. Bake for 10 to 12 minutes or until delicately browned.

Yield: 32 crescents.

Approximately 100 calories each.

Strawberry Almond Sunflower Squares

These delicate, fruity double deckers are an invitation to a cozy tête-à-tête, a prelude to a lovely evening!

¼ cup sunflower seeds,
    ground to a flour
¼ cup wheat germ
½ cup granola (see page 29)
2 tablespoons butter, melted
2 eggs, beaten

1 cup almonds, chopped
½ cup unsweetened strawberry
    preserves (Sorrell Ridge
    is a good brand)
1 teaspoon vanilla

Preheat oven to 325°F.

In a bowl, combine the sunflower flour, wheat germ, and granola. Add the melted butter and mix together.

In another bowl, mix together the beaten eggs, almonds, preserves, and vanilla.

Press one cup of the crumb mixture in an 8-inch-square baking pan lined with parchment paper or greased with a mixture of liquid lecithin and oil. Spoon the strawberry-almond mixture over the crumb crust and top with the remaining crumbs. Bake for 20 to 25 minutes. Cool slightly, then cut into 1-inch squares.

Yield: 25 squares.

Approximately 75 calories each.

11
FOUNTAIN
OF YOUTH COOKIES

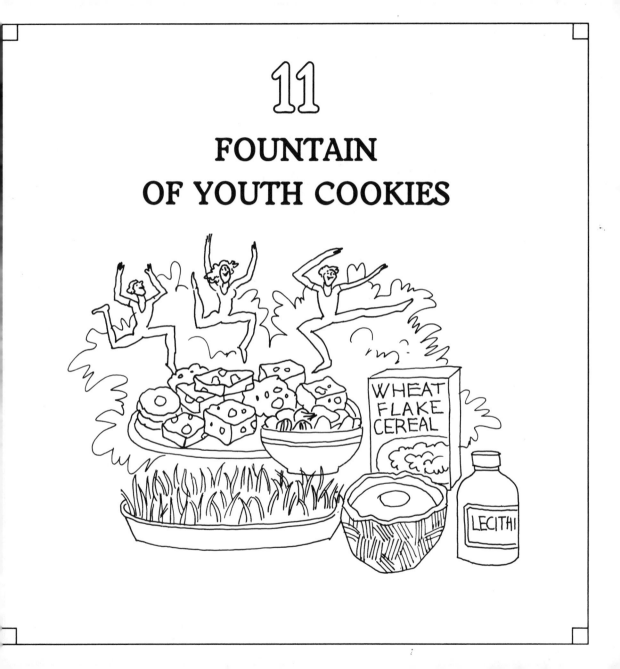

You can live it up and live longer if you give your body optimum nutrition, with more vitamins and minerals which, as you light more candles on your birthday cake, your body needs more but utilizes less.

How do you do that? By addition and subtraction. Subtract the foods that add only empty calories. Add the foods that give you important nutrients, and you will multiply your chances of enjoying all your years in the best of health.

The cookies in this chapter are fortified with ingredients that have been shown to sharpen the mind, lower LDL cholesterol (the bad kind), improve circulation, and promote restful sleep. The taste? Your whole family will label them winners.

Fruit and Nut Lifesavers

To stay young and vital, you should eat each day something which, if put into the ground, would grow. Sprouts, sunflower seeds, and sesame seeds would grow if planted, and this no-bake confection bring their vitality to you. The lecithin granules contribute to a sharp mind and a good memory.

12 dried apricots, soaked overnight
½ cup raisins, soaked overnight
apple juice (for soaking the apricots and raisins)
3 tablespoons almonds, lightly roasted
3 tablespoons rolled oats
3 tablespoons lecithin granules
3 tablespoons wheat germ
2 tablespoons bran

1 tablespoon dry milk powder
2 tablespoons wheat or rye sprouts (optional; see page 37)
2 tablespoons unsweetened shredded coconut
2 tablespoons sunflower seeds
3 tablespoons sesame seeds and toasted filberts for garnish

Soak the apricots and raisins overnight in apple juice.

Drain, and reserve the juice for fruit salad or drink it. (It's delicious.) In a food processor, blender, or food mill, puree the dried fruit, then blend with nuts, oats, lecithin, wheat germ, bran, milk powder, sprouts, coconut, and sunflower seeds. If the mixture is too sticky to handle, refrigerate for about an hour, or if you want to get on with it, add more oats.

Pinch off pieces the size of small walnuts, roll each into a ball, dip in sesame seeds, then press a filbert in the center.

Yield: 2 dozen.

Approximately 40 calories each.

Crunchy Fudgy Brownies

These moist, chewy brownies are sure to wow your family and friends. Besides being rich in fiber, they provide an extra bonus of lecithin, which is rich in choline, a substance that sharpens the mind and keeps the arteries clean.

⅓ cup vegetable oil (preferably olive)
⅓ cup honey
2 tablespoons lecithin granules
2 eggs
1 teaspoon vanilla
1 cup whole wheat pastry flour

2 tablespoons soy flour
¼ cup bran
2 tablespoons milk powder
½ cup carob powder
⅓ cup chopped walnuts
Grapenuts cereal, millet, and sesame seeds for garnish

Preheat oven to 325°F.

In food processor, blender, or mixing bowl, blend the oil, honey, lecithin, eggs, and vanilla until smooth and creamy. Add the combined flours, bran, and milk and carob powders, and process briefly until ingredients are well-mixed. Mix in the nuts.

Spoon into an 8-inch-square pan lined with parchment paper or greased with a mixture of liquid lecithin and oil. Top with 1½-inch-wide rows of (alternately) Grapenuts, millet, and sesame seeds. Bake for 20 to 25 minutes. Cut into 1½-inch squares.

Yield: 20 squares.

Approximately 100 calories each.

Mixed-Grain Peanut Almond Squares

The combination of oat and wheat provides complementary amino acids, thus increasing the biological value of the protein in these unbelievably delicious squares. You can use any combination of unsweetened dry cereals you have on hand.

1 tablespoon butter	¼ teaspoon ginger
1 tablespoon molasses	¼ teaspoon nutmeg
1 tablespoon honey	1 cup dry oat cereal, toasted
3 tablespoons frozen apple juice concentrate	1 cup dry wheat-flake cereal, toasted
3 tablespoons peanut butter	½ cup chopped almonds or peanuts, toasted
2 tablespoons lecithin granules	
½ teaspoon cinnamon	

In a saucepan, combine butter, molasses, honey, and apple juice. Heat and stir until ingredients are well-combined. Add the lecithin, spices, cereals, and nuts and mix.

Press the mixture into an 8-inch-square pan lined with parchment paper. Cool, then cut into 1-inch squares.
Yield: 25 squares.
Approximately 70 calories each.

Tranquility Tahini Fig and Nut Cookies

The tahini, oats, wheat germ, figs, and milk powder in these crisp and crunchy cookies provide bountiful calcium and magnesium, which have been shown to improve mental and physical functioning and promote restful slumber. They are an excellent bedtime snack.

¼ cup tahini
2 tablespoons vegetable oil (preferably olive)
2 tablespoons honey
½ cup rolled oats
¼ cup oat bran or wheat germ
1 tablespoon dry milk powder

4 dried figs soaked for at least an hour or overnight in hot water, then drained and cut into small pieces
¼ cup sunflower seeds or chopped walnuts

In a mixing bowl, combine the tahini, oil, and honey. Stir in the oats, bran, milk powder, figs, and seeds or nuts.

Preheat oven to 325°F.

Drop the batter by teaspoonfuls on a cookie sheet lined with parchment paper or greased with a mixture of a few drops of liquid lecithin and oil. Bake for 12 to 15 minutes, or until cookies are a delicate brown.

Yield: 20 to 24.

Approximately 45 calories each.

Apricot Walnut Shortbread Squares

You'll find it hard to believe that anything that tastes so scrumptious can do so many wonderful things for you—lecithin for your arteries and your memory, wheat germ for that great vitamin E, fiber for good digestion, apricots for iron, nuts for magnesium. Invite your best pal and enjoy them with a nice cup of tea.

BASE

½ cup whole wheat pastry
  flour
2 tablespoons wheat germ
2 tablespoons bran
2 tablespoons lecithin granules
2 tablespoons vegetable oil
  (preferably olive)

2 tablespoons butter
1 tablespoon honey
1 tablespoon frozen apple juice
  concentrate
½ teaspoon vanilla extract

FILLING

½ cup dried apricots soaked in
  ½ cup boiling water or
  Lemon Soother tea for at
  least an hour or
  overnight

2 tablespoons frozen apple
  juice concentrate
½ cup chopped walnuts

Soak the apricots in boiling water or Lemon Soother tea for at least one hour, or overnight.

Preheat oven to 325°F.

To make the base, blend together in food processor, blender, or mixing bowl all the ingredients, from the flour to the vanilla. Press ¾ cup of this mixture into an 8-inch-square pan lined with parchment paper or greased with a mixture of a few drops of liquid lecithin and oil. Bake for 15 minutes or until edges begin to turn brown.

To make the filling, combine the apricots with their soaking liquid and the apple juice concentrate in a saucepan, and cook over medium heat for about 10 minutes. Puree in food processor or blender, then add the chopped walnuts.

Spread the apricot mixture over the cookie base and top with the remaining ¼ cup of the crumb mixture. Return to oven for 10 to 15 minutes. Cool, then cut into 1½-inch squares.

Yield: 25 squares.

Approximately 55 calories each.

12
VERY SKINNY SMART COOKIES
For Calorie Counters

As I mentioned in the Introduction, all the cookies in this book are calorie-smart. They have much less fat and sweetening agents than their counterparts in the great big cookie world.

In this chapter, though, we reduce the calories even further by the use of popcorn flour, which has 50 calories to a cup as compared with regular flour's 400, and by the increased use of bran, which is not only ridiculously low in calories (6.7 to a tablespoon), but has a very accommodating way of slowing down the absorption of other calories. We also use fruit juices as a substitute for the more concentrated, more caloric sweeteners.

Nosh on these delicious morsels in good conscience. And serve them at teas, committee meetings, and parties. Your weight-watching friends will bless you.

Calorie-Shy Miniature Cheesecake Tarts

Enjoy your passion for cheesecake without guilt! Popcorn flour and orange juice enhance the flavors and slash the calories in these scrumptious, easy-to-make tarts.

BASE

    1 cup mashed banana   *1 cup popcorn flour*

FILLING

    ½ cup cottage cheese or ricotta   *1 tablespoon vanilla*
        cheese, drained   *fruit preserves (Sorrel Ridge*
    ⅓ cup cream cheese   *is a good brand) and*
    1 egg   *carob chips (optional)*
    3 tablespoons frozen orange
        juice concentrate

Line the 24 cups of two muffin tins with paper liners. Combine mashed banana with popcorn flour, and press a scant teaspoon of this into each of the cups.

Preheat oven to 350°F.

In food processor, blender, or mixing bowl, blend together the cheeses, egg, orange juice, and vanilla. Fill the paper cups halfway with the cheese mixture. Top with a small dollop (about ¼ teaspoon) of fruit preserves or a carob chip, if desired. Bake for 15 minutes.
Yield: 24 tarts.

Approximately 30 calories each without topping; 35 calories with topping.
Note that fruit preserves made with fruit juices as the only sweetener provide very few extra calories—the Sorrel Ridge brand contains only 14 per teaspoon.

Lemon Wafers

A refreshingly light cookie with a pleasant lemony flavor.

¼ cup unsalted (sweet) butter
¼ cup honey
1 egg
1 tablespoon lemon juice or extract
1 cup whole wheat pastry flour

¼ cup wheat germ
¼ cup bran
¼ teaspoon baking soda
1 teaspoon grated lemon rind

In food processor, blender, or mixing bowl, mix together the butter, honey, egg, and lemon juice. Add the combined flour, wheat germ, bran, baking soda, and lemon rind.

Preheat oven to 325°F.

Drop the batter by scant teaspoonfuls on a cookie sheet lined with parchment paper or greased with a mixture of a few drops of liquid lecithin and oil. Leave room for spreading.

Bake for 10 to 12 minutes or until they are delicately browned.

Yield: 50 cookies.

Approximately 25 calories each.

Orange-Bran-Nut Drops

Wholesome and flavorful—rich in protein, the B vitamins that give you an upbeat attitude, calcium, and potassium—these skinny cookies will light up your day!

¼ cup cream cheese
2 tablespoons frozen orange
　　juice concentrate
3 tablespoons honey
1 egg
½ cup yogurt
1 tablespoon grated orange
　　rind

2 teaspoons vanilla
1 cup whole wheat pastry
　　flour
½ teaspoon baking soda
½ cup bran
3 tablespoons wheat germ
½ cup chopped walnuts

In food processor, blender, or mixing bowl, blend together cream cheese, orange juice, honey, egg, yogurt, orange rind, and vanilla, until smooth and creamy. Mix in the combined flour, baking soda, bran, and wheat germ, and blend only until ingredients are combined. Mix in the nuts.

Preheat oven to 350°F.

Drop the batter by teaspoonfuls on a cookie sheet lined with parchment paper or greased with liquid lecithin and oil. Flatten the cookies slightly with a fork dipped in flour, and bake for 15 to 18 minutes.

Yield: 50 cookies.

Approximately 30 calories each.

Crunchy Sesame Cookies

A delightful nosh, reminiscent of the goodies from the old-fashioned candy store.

3 tablespoons vegetable oil
(preferably olive)
2 tablespoons honey
2 eggs

1½ cups sesame seeds, toasted
⅓ cup whole wheat pastry
flour
2 tablespoons wheat germ

Preheat oven to 325°F.

In food processor, blender, or mixing bowl, blend together the oil, honey, and eggs until smooth and creamy. Blend in the seeds, flour, and wheat germ. With wet hands, gather batter by pieces and roll into 1½-inch-long pieces about the thickness of a fountain pen. Place on cookie sheets lined with parchment paper or greased with a few drops of liquid lecithin and oil.

Bake for 15 to 18 minutes.

Yield: 55 cookies.

Approximately 40 calories each.

Carob Peanut Butter Meringues

A welcome taste diversion for anyone, but particularly good for those who cannot handle gluten or grains.

3 egg whites   *¼ cup honey*
¼ cup carob powder
¼ cup peanut butter (smooth
     or chunky)

In an electric mixer, beat egg whites until stiff. Add the carob powder and beat to incorporate. Beat in the peanut butter and then the honey.

Preheat oven to 300°F.

Drop the batter by teaspoonfuls on a cookie sheet lined with parchment paper or oiled with a mixture of liquid lecithin and oil. Bake for 10 to 12 minutes.

Yield: 36 cookies.

Approximately 25 calories each.

13

ENTERTAINING COOKIES
FOR GREAT CELEBRATIONS

Here are some sweet temptations you don't have to resist. Every crumb contributes to sociability!

For your big celebration, these cookies steal the show—each one is a mouth-watering picture. Arrange them tastefully on a doily-lined platter and they'll make a gorgeous centerpiece to delight the eye and titillate the taste buds.

Although they may look and taste positively wicked, there isn't an empty calorie in the lot. They contain no negative ingredients and are enriched to meet your high nutritional standards.

For a delicious taste of nostalgia, I have included recipes from different ethnic backgrounds so you can enjoy your culinary roots in good health.

Almond Kahlua Truffles

The ultimate taste treat! The rich, exotic coffee flavor of Kahlua blends with the crunch of toasted almonds and coconut to make an outrageously good, no-bake confection. Make double the recipe—they freeze well.

½ cup unblanched almonds, roasted

3 tablespoons carob powder plus 2 teaspoons (divided)

1 teaspoon instant coffee powder (regular, decaffeinated, or grain)

¼ cup shredded coconut

1 egg yolk

2 tablespoons Kahlua, plus 1 teaspoon

2 tablespoons toasted coconut

Roast the almonds in a 350°F oven for 10 minutes.

In food processor or blender, grind the almonds to the consistency of coarse crumbs. Add the 3 tablespoons of carob, the coffee, coconut, and egg yolk, and 2 tablespoons of the Kahlua. Blend until all ingredients are incorporated.

Scoop up about ½ teaspoon of the mixture at a time and roll between palms into a ball the size of a marble. Skewer on a toothpick, then roll each marble first in the remaining Kahlua, then in the remaining carob powder, and finally the toasted coconut. If you have any left after the usual raid by the kitchen kibitzers, refrigerate or freeze them until company comes.

Yield: 24 truffles.

Approximately 35 calories each.

Polynesian Fruit and Nut Squares

For that "I could have danced all night" feeling, try this treat. The fruit sugar provided by the pineapple and orange is quickly absorbed by the blood and carried to the muscle cells where it plays an energy-giving role.

2 tablespoons vegetable oil
   (preferably olive)
1 teaspoon vanilla
2 eggs
3 tablespoons frozen orange
   juice concentrate,
   slightly thawed
3 tablespoons unsweetened
   strawberry or raspberry
   preserves (Sorrell Ridge
   is a good brand)

½ cup whole wheat pastry
   flour
¼ cup wheat germ
½ cup rolled oats
½ cup chopped walnuts,
   toasted
¼ cup sunflower seeds, toasted
1 cup shredded coconut
1 can (20 ounces) crushed
   pineapple with juice
¼ cup sliced almonds

Preheat oven to 350°F.

    In food processor, blender, or mixing bowl, blend together the oil, vanilla, eggs, orange juice, and preserves. Process till smooth and creamy. Blend in the combined flour, wheat germ, and oats, then mix in the nuts, seeds, coconut, and pineapple with juice. Pour batter into a 9 × 15-inch baking dish lined with parchment paper or greased with a mixture of a few drops of liquid lecithin and oil. Top with

sliced almonds. Bake for 45 minutes or until golden brown. Cool slightly, then cut into 1½-inch squares.
Yield: 60 squares.
Approximately 35 calories each.

Cheesecake Squares

Sinfully good! These disappear so fast, maybe you should double the recipe.

CRUST

¾ cup whole wheat pastry
   flour
2 tablespoons soy flour
2 tablespoons wheat germ

¼ cup unsweetened shredded
   coconut
¼ cup butter, softened
½ cup chopped walnuts or
   pecans

FILLING

8 ounces cream cheese or
   ricotta (well-drained)
¼ cup honey
1 egg
2 tablespoons milk

1 tablespoon lemon juice
½ teaspoon vanilla
1 teaspoon grated lemon rind
a few gratings of nutmeg

Preheat oven to 325°F.

To make the crust: In a bowl, combine the flours, wheat germ, and coconut. Using a pastry blender or 2 knives, cut the butter into the coconut mixture. Add the chopped nuts. Reserve ¾ cup of this mixture for topping. Spread the remaining mixture over the bottom of an 8-inch-square baking dish lined with parchment paper or greased with a mixture of lecithin and oil. Bake for 12 to 15 minutes or until firm and a little brown around the edges.

To make the filling: In food processor or blender, blend together the cheese, honey, egg, milk, lemon juice, and vanilla until smooth and creamy. Mix in the grated rind and nutmeg. Pour the cheese mixture over the baked crust, top with remaining crumbs, and bake for another 30 minutes. Let cool slightly, then cut into 1-inch squares.
Yield: 32 squares.
Approximately 74 calories each with cream cheese; 60 calories with ricotta.

Raspberry Almond Maple Thins

A lovely marriage of flavors and textures, these meringue-topped thins with a raspberry filling and a sprinkle of crunchy almonds can be made ahead and frozen.

3 ounces cream cheese
1/4 cup unsalted (sweet) butter
2 tablespoons honey
1 egg, separated
1 cup whole wheat pastry flour
1/8 teaspoon cream of tartar

1/4 teaspoon vanilla
1 tablespoon maple syrup granules
1/2 cup unsweetened raspberry preserves (Sorrell Ridge is a good brand)
1/2 cup sliced almonds

In food processor, blender, or mixing bowl, blend cheese, butter, honey, and egg yolk until light and creamy. Stir in the flour to make a fairly stiff dough. Wrap dough in plastic wrap and refrigerate a few hours or overnight.

Preheat oven to 325°F.

Divide the dough into four portions. Spread portions on an ungreased cookie sheet and pat into 9 × 3-inch rectangles. Bake for 10 minutes.

In a small bowl, beat the egg white until foamy. Add the cream of tartar and vanilla and beat until stiff. Gradually beat in the maple syrup granules.

When the baked dough cools, spread it with raspberry preserves, top with the maple meringue, and then sprinkle the almond slices over all. Bake for another 10 minutes or until meringue is tinged with gold. Allow to cool slightly, then cut down the center of each strip, and cut across in one-inch slices.

Yield: 4 dozen.

Approximately 40 calories each.

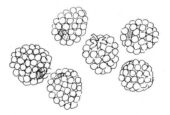

Cream Cheese Brownies

These delicious brownies will remind you of fudgy ice cream.

BROWNIE LAYER

2 eggs
1/4 cup unsalted (sweet) butter
1 tablespoon molasses
3 tablespoons honey
3 tablespoons frozen orange
    juice concentrate,
    slightly thawed

3 tablespoons Kahlua
1 cup whole wheat pastry
    flour
1 cup carob powder
1/2 cup unsweetened shredded
    coconut
1/2 cup toasted pecans

CHEESECAKE LAYER

2 eggs
8 ounces cream or ricotta
    cheese
2 tablespoons honey

2 tablespoons orange juice
    concentrate
1 tablespoon Kahlua or 1
    teaspoon vanilla

To make the brownie layer, blend together the eggs, butter, molasses, honey, orange juice, and Kahlua. Mix in the combined flour and carob powder. Blend to combine. Stir in the coconut and pecans; the batter will be thick.

Spoon the batter into a 9-inch-square pan lined with parchment paper or greased with a mixture of liquid lecithin and oil. Smooth batter into the pan. Set aside.

To make the cheesecake, blend together in food processor, blender, or mixing bowl the eggs, cheese, honey, orange juice, and Kahlua or vanilla. Blend until smooth and creamy.

Preheat oven to 325°F.

Pour the cheesecake mixture over the brownie mixture. With a wooden spoon, blend the two mixtures to make a marbleized or waterfall pattern. (For a fantastic variation, don't marbleize the brownie mixture with the cream cheese. Instead, use the cheese as a topping over the brownie base.)

Bake for about 40 minutes or until toothpick inserted in the center comes out clean. Cool, then cut into 1-inch blocks.

Yield: 4 dozen.

Approximately 65 calories for the cream cheese brownie; 53 calories with ricotta cheese.

Finnish Coffee Fingers

Crisp, flaky and light, they meet the tongue meltingly.

3 tablespoons unsalted (sweet) butter	1 cup whole wheat pastry flour
3 tablespoons cream cheese	¼ cup wheat germ
1 teaspoon almond extract	1 egg white, slightly beaten
3 tablespoons honey	½ cup finely chopped almonds

In food processor, blender, or mixing bowl, blend together the butter, cheese, almond extract, and honey until smooth and creamy. Add the flour and wheat germ, combined, and mix thoroughly. Refrigerate dough until well-chilled.

Preheat oven to 325°F.

Cut off small pieces of the chilled dough and roll between your hands into "fingers" about 2¼ inches long and ¼ inch in diameter. Dip cookies in the beaten egg white and then in the chopped almonds. Place on a cookie sheet lined with parchment paper or greased with a mixture of liquid lecithin and oil. Bake for 12 to 15 minutes, or until the cookies have a golden glow.

Yield: about 4 dozen.

Approximately 35 calories each.

Carob-Coated Ischl Sandwich Cookies

These confections are adapted from a version said to have been favored by Emperor Franz Joseph of Austria. They are named for the summer resort where he particularly liked to savor this heavenly indulgence.

2 tablespoons unsalted (sweet) butter
2 tablespoons cream cheese
½ cup ricotta cheese, drained
½ teaspoon lemon juice
1 teaspoon grated lemon zest (lemon peel)
¼ cup honey
1¼ cups whole wheat pastry flour
¼ cup wheat germ
2 tablespoons soy flour

1 teaspoon carob powder
½ teaspoon cinnamon
¼ cup jam or fruit preserves—apricot, strawberry, raspberry, or cherry orange marmalade (Sorrell Ridge is a good brand)
½ cup carob syrup (page 95) whole almonds, hazelnuts, or pecans for garnish (about ¼ cup)

Blend together in food processor, blender, or mixing bowl the butter, cheeses, lemon juice, zest, and honey until smooth and creamy. Add the combined flours, wheat germ, carob, and cinnamon and blend. Let the dough rest for about 15 minutes and then roll on a floured surface to ¼-inch thickness. Cut out cookies with a lightly floured 2-inch cookie cutter.

Preheat oven to 325°F.

Place cookies carefully on cookie sheets lined with parchment paper or greased with a mixture of liquid lecithin and oil.

Bake for 12 to 15 minutes or until golden. Watch carefully—they burn easily. Place cookies on rack to cool.

When cookies are cool, turn half of them upside down and spread about ½ teaspoon of jam on each. Make sandwiches with the other halves and set the cookies on a rack set over wax paper. Top each sandwich with ½ teaspoon of carob syrup, or enough to cover the top. Place a toasted almond, hazelnut, or pecan on each.

Yield: 30.

Approximately 60 calories each.

Strudel

Strudel is a measure of the high esteem in which you hold your guests. It is served on great occasions—weddings, engagement parties, bar mitzvahs, and celebrations in honor of outstanding achievement, such as an Emmy, an Oscar, a Nobel Prize, or a new baby.

Strudel dough can be made with whole wheat pastry flour, but it will not be quite so tender or "stretchy" as when made with unbleached white flour. If you choose to use the unbleached, you can compensate for its vitamin deficiencies by adding wheat germ to the filling, one tablespoon per each cup of flour (sprinkle it on the rolled and stretched dough).

The filling in this recipe calls for a grated orange and a grated lemon. That means you use the *whole* fruit, skin and pulp—everything except the seeds.

APRICOT FILLING

2 cups dried apricots
    hot water
¼ cup honey
1 whole lemon, grated and
    pitted

1 whole orange, grated and
    pitted

NUT MIXTURE

1 cup crushed walnuts
½ teaspoon cinnamon
1 cup raisins
½ cup cake, cookie, or graham
    cracker crumbs

½ cup finely ground wheat
    germ
1 cup unsweetened shredded
    coconut

STRUDEL DOUGH

1 egg
¼ cup vegetable oil (preferably
    olive)
6 tablespoons warm water
2 cups whole wheat pastry
    flour or unbleached
    white flour

vegetable oil (for drizzling
    over the dough)
ground walnuts (optional)

To prepare the filling, wash the apricots, then cover with hot water. Let them soak for a few hours or overnight. Drain off the water (it makes a delicious fruit juice). Chop the apricots fine; place in a bowl and add the honey. Using a food processor, blender, or mixing bowl, add half of the grated lemon and orange to the chopped fruit and

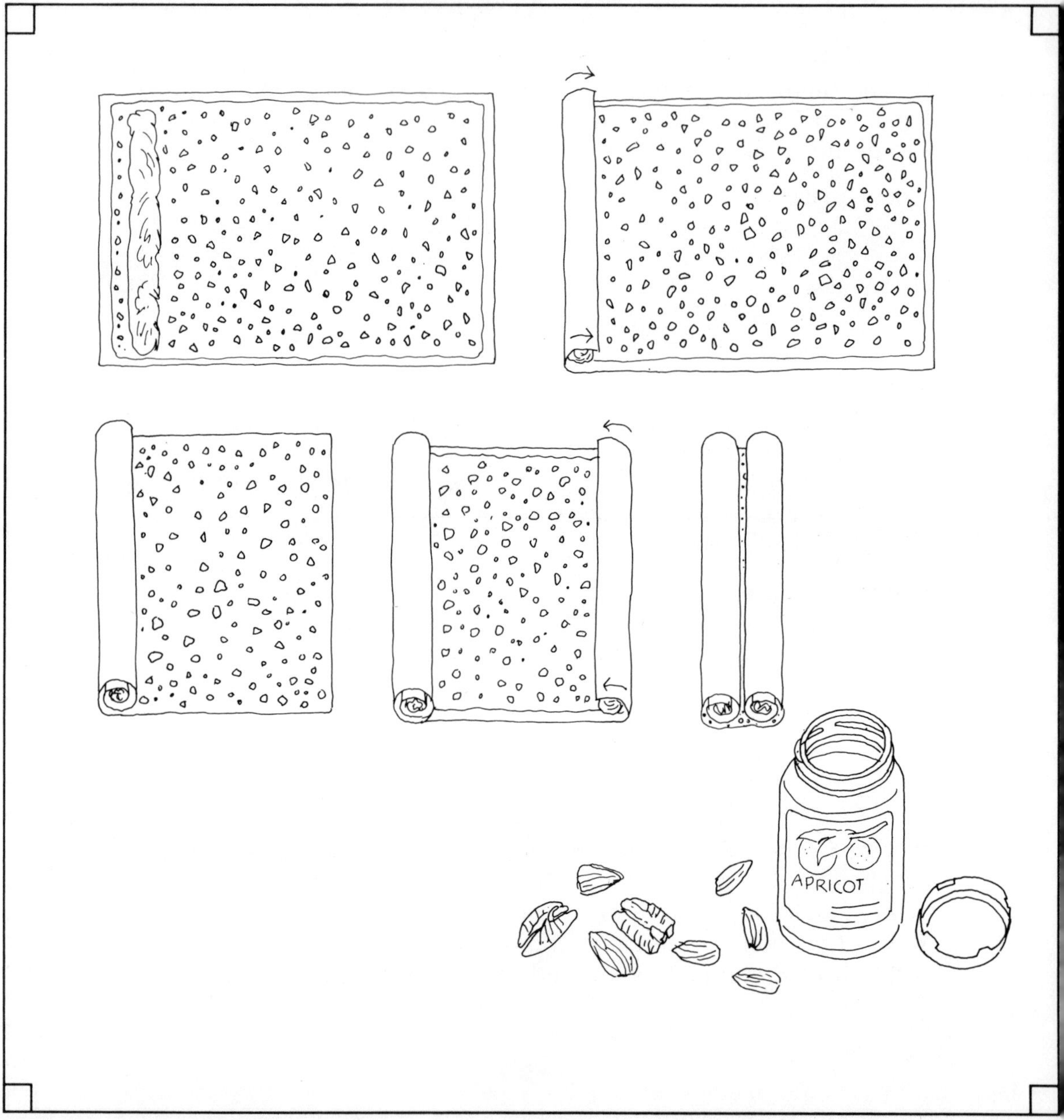
APRICOT

honey. Reserve the other half for use with the nut mixture. Although the apricot mixture makes a great filling, you may substitute any good-quality fruit preserve, preferably unsweetened. I like the Sorrell Ridge brand.

To make the nut mixture, combine the walnuts, cinnamon, raisins, crumbs, wheat germ, coconut, and the reserved grated lemon and orange.

To make the dough, beat the egg in a bowl. Add ¼ cup vegetable oil and the water, then the flour. Knead lightly until the dough is soft. Cover and set in a warm place for 1 hour.

Divide the dough in half. Place one half on a floured tablecloth and roll it out. Stretch and pull gently until it is as thin as tissue paper, or as thin as possible without tearing.

After the dough has been stretched as thin as possible, spread the nut mixture over the entire sheet. Drizzle a little oil over all. Spread ¼ of the fruit mixture in a thin line across one end of the sheet, about 3 inches from the edge. Fold this 3-inch edge over the fruit mixture, raise the tablecloth, and let the dough roll over itself to the halfway point. Follow the same procedure with the other side of the sheet. Roll out the second piece of dough and fill it in the same manner.

Place the rolls in a pan lined with parchment paper or greased with a mixture of liquid lecithin and oil. Brush with oil and dust with extra ground nuts, if desired. Let stand for about 15 minutes.

Preheat oven to 350°F.

Slice the strudel diagonally into 1-inch pieces, but do not cut all the way through. Bake for about 45 minutes. When cool, cut all the way through.

Yield: 20 pieces.

Approximately 140 calories each.

14
SMART COOKIES
FOR THE ALLERGIC

The foods that most commonly cause allergic reactions are cow's milk, corn, wheat, eggs, and chocolate. In this chapter I have created some special cookies that sidestep one or more of the common food allergies. In addition, consider the following suggestions when you are making Smart Cookies or other foods.

If you are allergic to milk, substitute herbal tea or fruit juice.

If you are allergic to corn and a recipe calls for cornstarch, substitute an equal amount of arrowroot or potato starch. Since most baking powders contain corn, make your own baking powder by combining ¼ teaspoon baking soda with ½ teaspoon cream of tartar. This is equivalent to 1 teaspoon of baking powder.

If you are allergic to eggs, you can achieve the emulsifying effect of one egg by combining 2 tablespoons whole wheat pastry flour, ½ teaspoon oil, ½ teaspoon baking powder, and 2 tablespoons milk, water, or fruit juice.

If you are allergic to wheat, eliminate the wheat germ and wheat bran. Substitute an equal amount of corn germ, oat bran, or rice polish.

Here are some substitutes for one cup of whole wheat flour: 1⅓ cups ground rolled oats; ⅝ cup rice flour, plus ⅓ cup rye flour; ½ cup potato flour, plus ½ cup rye flour; 1¼ cups rye flour; or ¾ cup rice flour, plus ½ cup amaranth flour.

Anise Drops

When you feel like eating something dairy-free, but you don't know just what, these nutrient-rich, fat-free Hungarian confections will fit the bill.

2 eggs
¼ cup honey
¼ teaspoon anise flavoring
1¼ cups whole wheat pastry flour

2 tablespoons soy flour
¼ cup wheat germ

In a food processor, blender, or mixing bowl, blend together the eggs, honey, and anise until smooth and creamy. Add the combined flours and wheat germ and mix to blend.

Drop the batter by teaspoonfuls on a cookie sheet lined with parchment paper or greased with a mixture of a few drops of liquid lecithin and a few drops of oil.

Set the cookie sheet, uncovered, in a cool place but not in the refrigerator, for about 8 hours or overnight.

Preheat oven to 325°F.

Bake for 6 to 7 minutes. Place cookies on a rack to cool.

The cookies will have a crisp crust and a cake-like interior.

Yield: 42.

Approximately 25 calories each.

Peanut Raisin Carob Chews

A delicious pick-up! Wheat, egg, and dairy free!

1 cup peanut butter   ¼ cup carob powder
¾ cup raisins   ½ teaspoon vanilla
¼ cup honey   1 cup finely chopped peanuts

Combine peanut butter, raisins, honey, carob, and vanilla. Mix and form into a dough. Pinch off clumps (about ¼ cup), and form into rolls 6 inches long and about 1 inch in diameter. Roll in chopped peanuts. Chill, then cut into slices about ¼-inch thick.

Variations: Instead of peanuts, roll in coconut, chopped sunflower seeds, or chopped nuts.

Yield: About 100 slices.

Approximately 30 calories each.

Carob Kahlua Cheesecake Tarts

No wheat, but a crunchy brownie base mingles with the creamy cheese and exotic Kahlua to delight your tastebuds.

CRUST

½ cup almonds, unblanched, roasted for 10 minutes in a 350°F oven
2 tablespoons carob powder

¼ cup unsweetened shredded coconut
2 tablespoons honey
2 tablespoons Kahlua

FILLING

8 ounces cream or ricotta cheese, or a combination
1 egg
2 tablespoons honey

1 teaspoon vanilla
2 tablespoons Kahlua
carob chips for garnish

To make the crust, combine almonds, carob, coconut, honey and Kahlua.

In food processor, blender, or mixing bowl, make the filling by blending together the cheese, egg, honey, vanilla, and Kahlua until smooth and creamy.

Line the cups of two muffin tins with paper liners (one dozen each). Place about a half teaspoon of the crust mixture in each and press down with the back of a spoon.

Preheat oven to 350°F.

Place a tablespoon of cheese mixture on the crust, and top with a carob chip. Bake for 20 minutes.

Yield: 2 dozen.

Approximately 70 calories each using cream cheese, 50 calories using ricotta cheese.

Amaretto Cheesecake Tarts

Just because you are allergic to wheat doesn't mean you cannot enjoy a divinely flavored cheesecake.

BOTTOM LAYER

⅓ cup sunflower seeds or almonds, ground fine

⅓ cup unsweetened shredded coconut

FILLING

8 ounces cream cheese

1 egg

2 tablespoons honey

2 tablespoons Amaretto liqueur

Line the cups of two muffin tins with paper liners (one dozen each). Combine sunflower seeds and coconut. Place 1 teaspoon of this mixture in each liner. Press down with the back of a spoon to cover the bottoms.

Preheat oven to 325°F.

To make the filling, cut the cream cheese into 8 blocks and blend with egg, honey, and Amaretto in food processor, blender, or mixing bowl till smooth and creamy. Place a tablespoon of the filling in each tartlet cup and bake for 15 minutes.

Yield: 2 dozen.

Approximately 60 calories each.

Tofu Cheeseless Tarts

No eggs, no wheat, no dairy foods—and favored even by those who can handle all of these. Almond-topped tofu tarts are high in protein and rich in dynamite nutrients, and though they are low in calories, they taste like a zillion!

FILLING

½ cup dried figs, cut up
(raisins may be
substituted)
½ cup apple juice
3 tablespoons orange juice
concentrate

1 teaspoon grated orange rind
2 tablespoons tahini
1 teaspoon vanilla
2 tablespoons honey
1 pound tofu, well drained
sliced almonds

CRUST

1 ripe banana
½ cup ground sunflower seeds
½ cup unsweetened shredded
coconut

½ teaspoon cinnamon
¼ teaspoon allspice

To make the filling, first drain the tofu by cutting it in cubes and placing the cubes on a folded dish towel. Place another towel on top. Place a cookie sheet or an oblong cutting board over all, then add about 3 pounds of weight. (Use jars of water or cans from the pantry.) Let stand for 10 to 15 minutes.

While the tofu is draining, cook the figs or raisins in the apple juice until they are soft—about 10 minutes. In food processor or blender, puree the fruit with the orange juice concentrate.

Add the orange rind, tahini, vanilla, honey, and drained tofu. Blend until smooth and creamy. Set aside.

To make the crust or bottom layer, mash the banana in a flat soup bowl. Add the ground sunflower seeds, coconut, cinnamon, and allspice.

Preheat oven to 350°F.

Line the cups of three muffin tins with paper liners (1 dozen in each). Place a teaspoon of the banana mixture in the bottom of each, and then a heaping tablespoon of tofu filling. Top each with sliced almonds.

Bake for 20 minutes.

Yield: 3 dozen.

Approximately 40 calories each.

The Ingredients
and Their Nutrients

Almonds   Excellent source of protein, potassium, iron, calcium, phosphorus, and essential fatty acids.

Amaranth   Not exactly a household word, but fast gaining popularity with American cooks. Amaranth is a plant food valued for its nutritious leaves and seeds, which are higher in protein than grains like wheat and rye. Because it is a plant food and not a grain, it is acceptable to those allergic to wheat or other grains.

Apricots   High source of vitamin A, and provides the B vitamin niacin, magnesium, calcium, phosphorus, and iron.

Bananas   Good source of potassium, some vitamin A, and vitamin C.

Barley Malt Syrup   Provides protein, calcium, and some B vitamins.

Bran   The outer coating of the wheat, corn, or rice grain, bran is a particularly good source of niacin, potassium, iron, phosphorus, calcium, and minerals, and it is high in fiber.

Buckwheat   Good source of protein, complex carbohydrates, and minerals.

Carob   Flour or powder is 8% protein and over 70% carbohydrate, and is an exceptionally good source of calcium and phosphorus.

Cashew Nuts   Good source of protein, potassium, phosphorus, calcium, and some iron.

Cheese, Ricotta   Sometimes called "Italian cottage cheese," this is higher in fat and calories than cottage cheese. One cup of ricotta made from whole milk contains about 430 calories and 32 grams of fat. When made

161

from part skim milk, it contains 340 calories and 19 grams of fat. A cup of creamed cottage cheese contains only 215 calories and 9 grams of fat.

Coconut Shreds   The meat of the coconut, dried, then shredded. An excellent sweetener that provides calcium, phosphorus, iron, potassium, and small amounts of the B vitamins.

Cornmeal (Hy-Lysine)   Made from corn containing higher levels of amino acids, especially lysine, which is usually low in grains. Most cornmeal is low in protein, but Hi-lysine provides protein of very high biological value, as well as iron, calcium, magnesium, potassium, B vitamins, and vitamin A.

Figs   Good source of potassium and magnesium, and provides some iron and B vitamins.

Honey   Provides some potassium, magnesium, calcium, and traces of the B vitamins.

Lecithin Granules   Derived from soybeans, they contain a rich supply of choline and inositol, which are members of the B-vitamin family and are essential to the production of lecithin and the utilization of fats.

Maple Syrup   A naturally occurring sweetener rich in minerals.

Millet   Provides protein and some B vitamins (especially thiamine).

Molasses, Blackstrap or Third Extraction   Excellent source of iron and calcium.

Oats or Rolled Oats   Provide potassium, calcium, iron, magnesium, zinc, and contribute a pleasant nutty flavor.

Orange Juice Concentrate   Provides potassium, phosphorus, calcium, magnesium, vitamins C and A, and traces of the B vitamins.

Peanut Butter   Crunchy or smooth, it furnishes protein, unsaturated fatty acids, minerals, and the B vitamin niacin.

Pecans Provide protein, unsaturated fatty acids, potassium, calcium, some iron, and traces of the B vitamins.

Pumpkin Seeds A good source of zinc.

Raisins Contain iron, calcium, potassium, magnesium, some vitamin B6, and traces of the other B vitamins.

Rice Flour Made from ground short-grain brown rice, this type of flour provides protein, potassium, magnesium, calcium, the B vitamins (notably niacin), and fiber.

Rice Syrup A sweetener made from brown rice, it provides protein, calcium, vitamins B1 (thiamine) and B2 (riboflavin), and a big dose of iron.

Sesame Seeds Provide unsaturated fatty acids, calcium, magnesium, phosphorus, and small amounts of vitamin A and the B vitamins.

Sorghum Syrup The concentrated juice of sorghum, a cereal grain related to corn; provides a smattering of iron, phosphorus, and calcium.

Soy Flour Made from ground soybeans, it has a high protein content (35%) and is also high in fat (20%). It's available with various degrees of fats removed and its amino acids complement those of wheat. Soy flour has no gluten, making it safe for those who cannot tolerate gluten, but it will not raise the bread.

Sunflower Seeds An excellent snack food, they are a powerhouse of nutrients, including protein, B vitamins, iron, phosphorus, calcium, and a highly digestible polyunsaturated oil.

Tahini Also known as sesame butter, it's rich in important linoleic acid, which helps the body utilize fats.

Tofu Derived from soybeans, and sometimes called soy cheese. A versatile protein food, rich in the B vitamin choline, minerals, and lecithin.

Walnuts Supply a good mix of all the important minerals, as well as vitamin A, the B-vitamin family, and vitamin C; also an excellent source of protein and essential fatty acids.

Wheat Germ   The heart of the wheat berry, it's tremendously nutritious—rich in protein, B vitamins, and vitamin E, and many minerals.

Whole Wheat Flour   Made from whole wheat berries with germ, bran, and endosperm (the white part) all intact, whole wheat flour is a good source of potassium, iron, vitamin B1 (thiamine), calcium, and protein.

Yeast, Brewer's or Nutritional   Excellent source of protein, the B vitamins, and many important minerals.

INDEX

167

Ask for these titles at your local bookstore or order today

Use this coupon or write to: Newmarket Press, 18 East 48th Street, New York, N.Y. 10017 (212) 832-3575:

Please send me:

Jane Kinderlehrer's SMART COOKIES: *80 Recipes for Heavenly, Healthful Snacking*
_____$9.95, paperback, 176 pages (ISBN 0-937858-62-5)

Jane Kinderlehrer's SMART MUFFINS: *83 Recipes for Heavenly, Healthful Eating*
_____$9.95, paperback, 176 pages (ISBN 0-937858-97-8)

For postage and handling, add $2.00 for the first book, plus $1.00 for each additional book. Please allow 4-6 weeks for delivery.

I enclose check or money order, payable to Newmarket Press, in the amount of $_____.

Name _____
Address _____
City/State/Zip _____

Clubs, firms, and other organizations may qualify for special discounts when ordering quantities of these titles. For more information, please call or write the Newmarket Special Sales Department at the above address.

BOB 038801-KIND.DM